GW00643827

Even Elvis

Even Elvis

by

Mary Ann Thornton

NEW LEAF PRESS, INC.
Harrison, Arkansas

First Printing, 1979

Cover design: Peter Hope

Library of Congress Catalog Card Number: 79-84343
International Standard Book Number: 0-89221-063-X

CONTENTS

Page

PREFACE

The question has been repeatedly asked if anyone reached Elvis Presley for God. If you will walk through four years of intricate precise guidance with me, introduced by a brief foundation for it, I'm sure you will find that God did send someone in His own perfect timing.

The entire theme of this testimony is God's love extending and extending to a man who was unique in many ways.

With our human eyes we saw him as either special or horrendous, based on our own personal opinions.

But through God's eyes he was loved with an everlasting love just as each of us are.

I have had the honor of accompanying Jesus of Nazareth as He went aside into "Samaria" to speak words of life to that particular soul.

I went to Elvis because the Lord sent me there, not simply because it was Elvis Presley. I also perceived God's grief and unbounded concern for Elvis. Not His anger.

Much has been stated about Elvis' quest for God . . . and his inability to find Him. While no one has revealed anything about how God loved, sought out, and found Elvis when his problems mounted.

Elvis' admitted unfulfilled call into an evangelistic ministry, his vast knowledge of God's Word, and the inner strugglings between the King of kings and the man the world proclaimed the "King of Rock" are explored within these pages with the intent that it would be an injustice to let this side of Elvis' search remain unrevealed.

To sum everything up in as few words as possible, I have to stand back with the realization that God's love is limitless to each of us and yet say, "Behold, how He loved him" (John 11:38).

—Mary Ann Thornton

"Call unto me, and I will answer thee, and show thee great and mighty things, which thou knowest not."

—Jeremiah 33:3

1

THE POTTER'S CLAY

"This child shall know two kingdoms in her lifetime," was the prophetic forecast given to me during the seventh week of my life by a radiantly beautiful, yet ancient-looking messenger. After delivering this message to my mother she vanished never to be seen again, but her words were accepted as an answer to the many times Mother had asked God to use my life for His glory.

In retrospect, I realize that God's intervention in my life at such an early age is what began the series of events that led me to the threshold of two separate and distinct kingdoms.

To provide a proper basis for the story, allow me to mention several things that caused me to become increasingly aware that a divine plan was in operation.

I vividly recall my first reactions to Elvis as I watched him perform on television in the fifties. Outwardly, it was one of amusement at his facial contortions and stage antics, while inwardly I sensed that our paths would cross one day. But that was ridiculous. After all, I was only seven years old, and it was apparent that we shared no common interests.

Shortly after Elvis became nationally known, Marie, a friend, proudly showed me a picture of him that she had purchased. I responded with a passive, "So what," and subdued the undeniable impulse that had surfaced from two years earlier.

Several months later, Marie and I convinced our mothers to take us to see "Flaming Star," a movie starring Elvis. I came home with the same premonition I'd had for six years.

The next reaction came as I played Elvis' "Blue Hawaii" album on the stereo I'd received on my fourteenth birthday.

My dad walked into my room impatiently demanding, "You'd

11

just as well forget about that record . . . and him! You'll never see him anyway."

Breaking my normal silence while being reprimanded, I replied, "Oh, yes, I will! I don't know when or where yet, but one of these days Elvis and I are going to lock horns over something."

Dad slowly walked away and I stood startled over the unfounded claim I had just made.

During the next two years, I met and began dating Jerry, who is now my husband. Neither of us were Christians at the time, so consequently his mother began praying for us.

I didn't believe people expected answers to their "spiritual exercises" so I wasn't worried about her constant petitions.

However, the Lord answered her prayers the night that Jerry and I attended Bud Chambers' tent revival with her.

Before the first song had been finished I'd knelt and accepted Christ as my Saviour.

Jerry's mother began immediately telling me that I'd probably be an evangelist one day. So I took an early retirement from Christianity in case she was right.

The next few years produced a husband, Jerry, and two daughters. Then in 1971, we decided to take our vacation in Tennessee and God decided to begin intervening in our lives again!

The first stop on our trip was Graceland, Elvis' home in Memphis.

As we approached the gates, they opened voluntarily. When cautiously approaching the drive, a guard came driving down from the mansion.

"Get in and I'll drive you up to the house," he offered.

Jerry and I looked at each other and got in the vehicle for the short ride.

"I'll be back to get you in a little while. I'm Mike McGregor. I work for Elvis," he added.

Then, suddenly, I glanced up to see Elvis watching us from a second floor window.

He obviously didn't want to be discovered, so rather than be conspicuous, I continued taking pictures and ignored him.

Although, on the way out I couldn't resist alerting Mike by saying, "By the way, tell Elvis that Mary Ann was here," and surprised myself by spontaneously adding, "and tell him that I'll definitely be back."

As Jerry and I walked toward the car I explained, "I don't know why I said that. Elvis doesn't have any idea who I am!"

12

After leaving Memphis for the remainder of our drive to the Smoky Mountains we repeatedly resisted an urge to return home. A feeling of impending danger seemed to hover in the air as we began the slow incline into the highlands.

The intensity of the situation increased when Jayne Ann, our four-year-old excitedly exclaimed, "I'm going up the mountain to meet Jesus!"

That seemed a profound statement since she hadn't been in Sunday school but three times in her life: Jerry and I looked at each other self-consciously, but neither of us had the courage to admit we weren't ready to "meet Jesus."

The steadily-falling rain had begun creating a slippery surface on the pavement as we approached a series of curves in the highway. As we rounded a bend I felt an impression to say, "Pull over to your side of the road as far as you can in case someone tries to push us off the mountain!" Then as I looked up, a station wagon slid into our lane and collided with us, causing our car to come to rest only a few inches from a 200-foot cliff. Jayne Ann's casual remark had nearly been prophetic. Miraculously, none of us was injured and assistance came in a way only God could have arranged. We began our journey home within hours, shaken and thinking.

In November, 1971, Elvis performed in Kansas City for the first time since the early years of his career. Coincidentally, this would be the second time in two months that our paths had crossed. Our dormant interest in Elvis began to gain renewed momentum.

Needless to say, we attended the concert. Midway through the show as Elvis sang, "How Great Thou Art," the Lord whispered, "Mary Ann, Elvis needs Me." I nodded in tearful agreement that Elvis did need Him, but I refrained from probing into a solution to the problem.

Shortly after Elvis' concert an advertisement was placed in the *Kansas City Star* requesting people to write and ask Elvis back again. After reading it Jerry suggested, "Why don't you write, too?"

"Really?" I answered, and within minutes began composing a brief note that sent me searching through a Bible for Scriptures to explain to Elvis Aaron Presley how he could become a priest for the Lord like another Aaron had been during Moses' time. After several strenuous hours passed by the letter was four pages long, and I still hadn't asked him to come back to Kansas City.

Less than five months later I became suddenly ill. A pain in my side had increased in intensity throughout the day until by the time Jerry came in from work I was screaming for relief. His first reaction was to ask his mother for prayer, but I made it clear that I didn't want prayer. So on ice-covered highways we drove to three separate clinics.

Each Doctor that examined me warned of impending surgery and filled out prescriptions that I systematically ripped into shreds! I knew the pills wouldn't help because each time I had walked into a different examination room the entire area of pain relocated.

"Just let me die and go to hell and get it over with!" I angrily demanded of Jerry on the way home. "I know better than anyone else that God is the One behind all of this. And furthermore, I'm *not* going to change!"

Midnight brought a worsening of my condition and Jerry called his mother to ask her to begin praying.

Three times during that night I recall slowly lifting my arms and body upward to a near-sitting position. I knew the pains I'd been having would prevent me from being able to apply pressure in these areas. However, there was no pain. Each time I reached the upright position, a man standing to my left would very gently and firmly lower my arms and body to their reclining state.

Minutes before Jerry left for work the following morning I made a point of thanking him for keeping me calmed during the night hours.

All his preoccupation of preparing to leave departed as he curiously replied, "But I wasn't up last night. I slept soundly all night long. If someone helped, it wasn't me."

We both immediately knew Who it was. Only Jesus loves enough to minister to those who denounce Him openly.

During the course of the next few days God healed me. And I was grateful, but not grateful enough to commit myself by going to church.

In the meantime, a local Assembly of God pastor had begun visiting us. He didn't need to talk about God, his presence alone reminded us of our spiritual conditions.

Pressures continued mounting and then, Sandy, Jerry's sister, came to ask us if Elvis' home in Memphis had double doors. We assured her that there was only one front door and then listened while she explained the reason behind her curiosity.

"Last night I had a strange dream of a white-columned building with huge double doors. I was standing in front of it wearing a glistening white robe, something that might be worn in Heaven. Elvis' presence seemed so real that I just assumed it was Graceland. Since you had been there, I thought I'd ask you and be sure. While that scene faded, a feeling of peace and well-being descended as the Lord's voice affirmed, 'Elvis will be saved'."

After discussing it, we were still baffled as to why the Lord would tell us something like this when we weren't saved either.

Within weeks Jerry's job was threatened by a layoff. Again we called his mother for prayer concerning a different job. After praying she received a Scripture giving instruction instead of an answer. The Scripture read, "But seek ye first the kingdom of God . . . and all these things will be added unto you" (Matt. 6:33).

Earlier, the same day, Jerry and I had each received the same Scripture. He didn't get the job then, but after we were "seeking the kingdom" the Lord granted the request.

We realized we had to turn to God. There wasn't any place else left to go and the only place we knew we were welcome was the Adrian Assembly of God Church with the persistent pastor.

The following Sunday, as we started for morning services, I stopped at the door, sighed and moaned, "Well, if you have to, then you have to!" And with that cheery attitude we prepared to surrender.

During the drive to church I'd decided I wasn't going to give up very easily, so I bravely resisted the altar call that was given that day.

The next Sunday the Lord chose to add a solemn warning through a prophecy stating, "You have honored Me with your mouth and your finances, but your heart is far from Me. If you don't turn to Me quickly the door will be shut!"

And for the second time I managed to walk out without repenting. I decided since I hadn't been struck down by a lightning bolt that I'd probably have another chance.

That chance came on August 19, 1973, when Jerry's parents were in church with us. As the sermon concluded I reached for his mother's hand to take her to the altar with me. But I missed, because she had been simultaneously reaching for mine!

I walked briskly to the altar, and as I knelt to ask forgiveness, the Lord quickly interjected, "Lay him down." I hadn't even had time to repent before the message had come! But the Lord didn't have to say names or explain further, I knew it was Elvis. However, I sensed that His request had come for a specific purpose.

Praying aloud in public services wasn't something I was very experienced in after only one week of being saved. However, our pastor wasn't one to let a person sit idle, so during the next week's meeting he requested that I pray aloud at the beginning of a church service. Endeavoring to do my best, I requested, "Lord, burden our hearts for the unsaved." I closed the prayer, satisfied that I hadn't sounded like a novice when the Lord unexpectedly requested, "Pray for Sandy (Jerry's sister) and Elvis Presley."

"No!" I firmly replied. Total silence followed. I couldn't tolerate that, so I began reasoning, "Lord, You asked me to 'lay Elvis down on the altar' a week ago. Go find someone else to do it! Don't You realize what I'd have to go through? Even at home!"

"Yes," came His calm answer.

"Well, then do You care enough about me to find someone else and leave me alone?" I nervously questioned, doubting His concern for my own happiness.

"No," was His understanding reply. Isn't it amazing what the Lord can convey in only one word?

"Okay, which one first? Elvis or Sandy?" I asked. As Sandy's name repeatedly ran through my mind I realized I'd accepted a task. Within four days she had given her life to Christ.

During the years I'd run from God I'd sensed it was from something as well as Someone. I was right. Elvis was next.

2

HIS FOOTSTEPS LED THE WAY

Nebuchadnezzar in the Book of Daniel was the scriptural example the Lord suggested as a guide concerning praying for Elvis. Reading it and seeing a man turn to God gave me the encouragement to proceed. And proceed I did! Most of my afternoons from that time forward included several hours of intercessory prayer for him.

I realized I'd have to start talking to people around Elvis sooner or later, although I was probably the last one to believe that I'd ever talk to Elvis personally. Anyone who knew the strict security surrounding him would completely agree!

The first logical impression I received was to reach someone who knew Elvis *as* Elvis instead of as a superstar. I eventually remembered the name of a family friend of the Presley's in their hometown of Tupelo, Mississippi. I phoned her and explained my position. She offered her prayers and suggested I try to contact Elvis at Baptist Memorial Hospital in Memphis. There'd been no press releases concerning his hospitalization yet, so this was news to me.

You can't imagine the giggly comments I received when I called the hospital and asked to talk to Elvis. Permission was denied, but the administrator's office gave me a detailed account of his illness and assured me that Elvis' health would have restricted any conversation. However, they assured me that the message I'd given them for him would be delivered immediately.

Later, that day I wrote a note of encouragement in a book of inspirational poetry and mailed it to Elvis.

During Elvis' concert in 1971, Jerry had recognized one member of the group and began suggesting that I contact him to find out how Elvis was feeling.

Taking his advice I phoned Hal's office and asked to speak with him. (Hal isn't his real name, but to retain his privacy, I'll address him by that name throughout the story.)

As he answered the phone, I exclaimed, "Praise the Lord! I finally found someone to talk to!" and then in a quieter voice added, "How is Elvis now?"

"Fine," came his not-so-convincing reply.

"I sent Elvis a book of poetry and called to tell him I was praying. Did he get the book?" I inquired as I gave Hal a description of it.

"Yes, he has it. I even remember seeing him lay it on his bedside table after he had been reading the poems," he answered in a surprised tone. "Do you realize what the odds were of even reaching him with a card?"

"No," I replied.

"The mail flow was over 5,000 articles daily," Hal announced. "So your chances were five thousand to one!"

I disagreed, the Lord had intended for that book to reach Elvis, so there weren't any odds.

"When I tell anyone that I'm praying for Elvis they laugh at me," I confided.

"Let them alone," Hal advised, "they laughed at Joshua too, but the walls of Jericho fell anyway."

I said good-by with the feeling that I had been accepted as a friend.

Within a few days of our conversation I received a note from Elvis thanking me for my prayers. So I had reached him after all!

Each time the altar at church was opened for prayer I knelt where the Lord had first asked me to pray for Elvis and poured out my requests.

One particular Sunday, a lady who knew nothing about my interest in reaching him came to me explaining, "Mary Ann, the Lord asked me to tell you something. You have a special work to do. You'll have to go through some fiery furnace trials and some lion's den experiences. Everyone is going to laugh at you, ridicule you, and say you're crazy, but if you keep looking up and keep your eyes on God you'll get the job done."

Those words proved true many times during the following months. I'm sure if the Lord hadn't given me this message I would have had trouble understanding some of the things that happened.

I realized that I couldn't discuss Elvis openly, and to reinforce that theory further, the Lord repeatedly gave part of Matthew 6:7 which states: "When thou prayest enter into thy closet . . . and thy Father which seeth in secret shall reward thee openly."

It seemed that everywhere I turned for several weeks, someone was either quoting this Scripture, giving it to me in the form of unsolicited advice, or I was opening my Bible to that particular passage of the gospels.

As the days passed, I began to look for tangible evidence that Elvis was changing instead of seeing the answers to my prayers by faith. As a result I became discouraged. After all, it had been three months and that should have been long enough to wait.

I still hadn't learned that God works His plan through love and patience within the heart of man before it spirals outward in the form of evidence.

During this period of enthusiastic desperation I foolishly demanded that the Lord allow the chandelier in the entry hall to move if Elvis was going to be reached. The Lord didn't reprimand me, He simply allowed me to stare at the light for over twenty minutes until I realized I was acting ridiculous before He steadily said, "Wait for something worthwhile." I received a partial answer, so I waited.

The next morning Jerry's sister, Sandy, called to ask if we would attend church with her that evening. Before we left their house, her husband, who wasn't a Christian, suddenly decided to go too.

After the service ended everyone was asked to kneel and pray. As I bowed my head the Lord suggested, "This is worthwhile."

"What's worthwhile?" I questioned.

His answer was to imprint my brother-in-law's name on my mind.

Realizing that He was referring to the previous day's conversation I replied, "All right, Lord, if You're going to find a way to get Elvis into Heaven, then don't allow my brother-in-law to leave this church tonight without going to the altar and asking for forgiveness."

"Get up and go to him," the Lord replied.

Approaching him I requested, "Would you go to the altar and pray with me?"

"No," came his cold reply. I closed my eyes and began weeping, because of the two negative answers I'd received. One from him and one from God.

19

"Okay, let's go," he added, grasping my arm to lead me away.

"Lord! He's dragging me out of this church in front of everyone," I moaned. "Am I so stubborn that it took something this drastic to get me to realize that Elvis can't be reached?"

Then, as he unexpectedly turned toward the altar, I opened my eyes to see that *he* was taking *me* to the altar instead of the other way around! This was definitely worthwhile! My brother-in-law accepted Christ, and the Lord had shown me that Elvis could be reached.

In answer to a continuing request for some of Elvis' group to appear in Kansas City, part of his travelling show had a New Year's Eve concert scheduled here. The weather restricted us from attending, so I asked the Lord to send someone to ask Hal the questions I'd wanted to ask.

Not only did He send someone, but it was taped for replay on a gospel radio station.

After I'd listened to the answers to my curiosities, one last question was asked, "Did Elvis ever mention touring with Jimmy Snow?"

"Yes, Elvis did say something like that," Hal replied.

I didn't know who Jimmy Snow was, but it seemed the Lord wanted me to know about him for a reason.

After the broadcast I began contemplating the impossible road that awaited me. I leaned back with a sigh, casually asking, "How long, Lord? How long?"

His immediate and unexpected answer was in the form of the first vision in a series giving me guidance through the completion of the assignment.

Suddenly, I found myself studying a long row of mountain peaks. Calculating the distance between them before progressing, I cautiously stepped from one to another. As my travelling continued, I stopped to look down, finding nothing but deep black valleys.

"Don't look down," came the Lord's unsolicited reply.

I continued treading upon the peaks until my curiosity began persuading me to look back. As I slowly turned my head, an immense hollow darkness was all that awaited my gaze.

"Don't look back either," was the Lord's gentle advice.

I obediently turned to complete my course, and after stepping across several more crevices I suddenly discovered that the row of summits had abruptly ended and I had stepped directly into a valley that was level with the peaks I had been walking upon.

The awesome height of these steep mountains flanking the valley illustrated to me that they were also insurmountable. I stood in the darkness of the valley contemplating my situation until a beam of light began gently urging me to look upward.

Ascending from this low place was a "transparent" gold stairway leading to a pair of white-pillared gates that were surrounded by white billowy clouds. The brightness of the scene was blinding in contrast to the darkness that was below and behind me. As the vision ended, I had been infused with the knowledge that finishing my course would include a long and tedious journey ending in victory.

Out of inquisitiveness I purchased a book relating Johnny Cash's testimony because he shared the same profession as Elvis.

A Rev. *Billy* Snow had been mentioned on the cover. It hadn't occurred to me that it was a misprint, but as I read I saw that Elvis and *Jimmy* Snow's names ran through it like threads in a tapestry.

I promptly phoned Rev. Snow at his church in Nashville to request his prayers. He was out, but returned my call that evening. We discussed Elvis at length and I discovered that Rev. Snow had known Elvis for years and had recently tried to talk to him. He compared his unsuccessful efforts to penetrate the security with "trying to get through the Gestapo!"

I gasped, and we ended our conversation agreeing to pray together for Elvis.

3

VISIONS AND VISITATIONS

Guidance had been given to the point of being unable to deny the commission. Even a brief glance at my past seemed to reflect that this wasn't a spontaneous second thought on the Lord's part. He had been gently leading me to this place. Why me? I asked many times, and I still don't know the answer. But I do know that God placed a faith and assurance inside of me that told me I could sit down and rationally and logically reason with Elvis as Jesus would do if He were here. I no longer saw Elvis as an entertainer or a public figure, instead he was a human being with unsolved problems, unhealed hurts, and unfulfilled desires. The very type of person Jesus came to minister to.

It seemed that during the past few weeks the name of a local Bible teacher with a well-proven prophetic ministry had been mentioned wherever we were.

When he was scheduled to speak at a church in our area, Jerry and I felt we should attend.

That night after finishing his message the speaker turned toward me, revealing, "The Lord would say unto you, 'I've heard your weeping and travailing in your secret place. It comes up to Me in the form of sweet incense of a sacrifice. I have heard your prayers and I *will* answer you. Yes, you have been called in accordance with My divine will and you will receive a divine visitation soon!' "

His prophecy had confirmed that I was totally within God's will, including being called. And the divine visitation was an answer to why I'd been sensing an intensifying presence of the Lord when I prayed.

I walked out of the church that night humbled and expectant.

Within the past seven months I had been constantly praying for the Lord to send Elvis back to Kansas City for another concert. At least I could get into the same room with him, and possibly we would be able to communicate to some degree.

In April, a concert announcement was made in regard to a performance by Elvis in Kansas City on June 29, 1974. I ordered two tickets and awaited God's instructions concerning my attendance.

The following Wednesday night as I signified my usual presence at an educational department staff meeting, the Lord informed me that I wouldn't be able to attend, because I'd be in the city. Since the Lord was interrupting my regular church-related activities, I assumed it was something about Elvis, my only extracurricular activity.

The Lord's plan was revealed when I was invited to hear Nicky Cruz' testimony at a rally in Kansas City on the night of the church meeting.

As Nicky began his story, I asked the Lord to allow him to mention Elvis' name if I was to request prayer from him like I had from Rev. Snow.

Instantly Nicky interjected, "That was back during the days that Elvis Presley was rockin' and rollin' and Lovin' 'em Tender."

I had received the proof I had requested, so after the conclusion of the rally, I walked backstage to find Nicky. What seemed to be a fruitless search ended when I turned to find him standing beside me!

"Elvis will be in Kansas City in a few weeks," I said. "Will you help me pray for him?"

"Certainly, let's pray right now," he readily suggested.

As we joined hands to pray, the Holy Spirit's presence descended in such an approving way that tears began trickling down my cheeks.

"Thank you," I replied as I walked away. "Keep praying for him, please."

"I will," he stated with a smile. "I will."

Prior to Elvis' concert Jerry had been praying for the Lord's presence during the performance.

Three days before the scheduled date the Lord confidently assured him that his prayers would be answered by explaining, "It will look as if a light is shining on Mary Ann all evening."

On the same day the Lord instructed me to open my Bible and read Isaiah 60:1-2, KJV. His message stated, "Arise, shine;

for thy light is come, and the glory of the Lord is risen upon thee. . . . darkness shall cover the earth, and gross darkness the people: but the Lord shall arise upon thee, and his glory shall be seen upon thee."

The verses related to the concert. I had known that when He asked me to read them. While the "darkness covering the earth" related directly to night and "gross darkness the people" told me of a dark room, and, of course, a concert hall is darkened except for the spotlights on the performers. So I had the sssurance that God would bless my attendance at the show, but I didn't realize for over two years just *how much* He blessed it!

During my devotions that morning of Elvis' arrival in Kansas City I was impressed to look up. Glancing toward the ceiling, I saw, in its place that same "transparent" gold stairway leading to Heaven. What had previously appeared to be white billowy clouds in the earlier similar vision had now revealed themselves to be literal clouds of angels! The white gates that were closed had been opened to disclose the Lord standing at the door, with His hands outstretched, while He looked down in smiling approval.

In the midst of a terrific storm Jesus began a journey down the first three steps and nearly completed the fourth before the vision ended. Many times I wondered if He ever touched that fourth step. He didn't—the meaning became clear when Elvis died three days before the fourth year would have begun.

Although the vision was over, the power and majesty of God lingered in the room, washing me in His peace and consolation. And again His vivid illustrations were self-explanatory.

The opened door told me that my "knocking" had been heard. The storm told me of a need for perseverance in the midst of buffeting and trial. While His outstretched arms assured His blessings and His descension to the fourth step reflected His increasing nearness.

I had scheduled a counselling session with my pastor the afternoon before the concert. Apprehension and a feeling of great responsibility gripped me as I drove to his office. Once I arrived I began pouring out my inner feelings, "I'd quit now rather than do the wrong thing. I know how important this is and I know the importance of reaching a soul with the Gospel. I know God is guiding me. I don't know why He doesn't use someone of more importance than I, but . . ."

"Wait a minute," he cautioned, "God uses willing vessels. Not personalities."

"Of course, you're right," I quickly replied, still unable to grasp that He trusted me with a specific task. "But pray for me, I don't want to fail God or Elvis."

"After the way you've been praying, the Lord isn't going to let you go to that concert without doing something," he assured. "Elvis will at least look, feel your prayers, say something, point toward you, or maybe, even a light will be shining on you during the evening. Just go and trust God because you'd be surprised at how many well-meaning Christians would condemn him to hell and go on their own way."

Jerry and I drove into the city early on the day of the concert. After we parked the car we sat down in a garden area only to look up and see Hal and Elvis staring at us from the Holiday Inn.

As Jerry and I walked to the hotel for lunch, the Lord drew my attention to the house phones by confidently informing me, "You'll be paged to those phones one day."

I didn't question Him, but I did wonder why He hadn't said, *today*, since Elvis and Hal were upstairs and had already seen us.

That evening after we had filed into the arena I left Jerry to buy refreshments. Through a series of wrong turns on the way to the refreshment stand I wound up near the backstage area. I knew no one would want me this close to Elvis, but apparently the Lord had led me here for a reason, so I knocked on the dividing partition and asked a guard if he would find Hal.

Within a few seconds Hal came over to me asking, "Can I help you?"

"Yes, I'm Mary Ann Thornton," I said, "and I called you."

"Today?" he questioned.

"No . . . last November," I said, and waited.

His facial expression began changing as he recalled our conversation. "Oh, yes . . . I do remember . . . the whole thing," he reflected.

I assured him that the Lord had sent me to the concert, and then he told me that I couldn't ever talk to Elvis.

Spontaneously, I stressed, "He's dying . . . he's dying . . . Oh, God, he's dying. Can't you see that? Somebody has to help him. Don't you know that? Can't you understand?"

As I spoke, my words had seemed rash and unrehearsed, although an inner assurance told me I'd spoken correctly.

"There's nothing I can do to help him," Hal replied, in a tone that made me sound hysterical, while the tears from his eyes betrayed his own words.

25

"If you can't help him, let me. I only want to reason with him," I pleaded.

Without answering me, Hal patted my head and walked away.

Gathering my emotions I walked back to explain to Jerry what had happened. Then, glancing back toward the stage, I saw for myself precisely why Hal couldn't help Elvis. He needed help himself!

After I told Jerry that someone had to do something I took a book on the Second Coming that I'd brought for Elvis, and returned to the backstage area.

For the second time, I received the guard's attention. Holding out the book for his inspection I asked, "Will you give this to Elvis?"

"I don't think Elvis would be interested," he stated, slamming the partition in my face.

I leaned against the wall in total defeat. I couldn't even get a book to him anymore.

Sensing a Divine presence, I lowered my head, reasoning, "Lord, if they're standing over there . . . then why aren't they over here helping me?"

Then slowly raising my eyes to look toward the hall I'd walked down earlier, I saw two angels, both looking satisfied that all was well, yet warning me not to return to my seat.

Turning back around, I glanced through a gap between the partitions and saw Elvis standing by the stage door.

As the orchestra played "2001: A Space Odyssey," his introduction, I called to him.

Nervously looking toward me each time I said his name, he seemed to question whether he should walk over to me or not.

After he abruptly entered the auditorium to begin his show, the Lord led me through a doorway telling me, "There's Elvis' Dad. Go talk to him and give him the book for Elvis."

I was unable to find him until I strained to look across the crowd. I walked briskly over to Vernon, introduced myself, and handed the book to him with an explanation.

After a lengthy conversation I gave him the same message I'd given to Hal. That Elvis wasn't going to live long.

Before I walked back to my seat, I stopped long enough to watch Elvis, before I needed binoculars.

As I watched him, it dawned on me to pray a few moments

26

before I left. After all, I'd been praying at a distance for several months. So why not pray where I could see the effects?

No sooner had I breathed a simple phrase when Elvis spun around on his heels and looked directly at me. Not around me, or in the vicinity, but *at me*, as if I had called his name.

That began a series of second looks that continued through the remainder of the evening.

Although, I realized God was moving, I didn't understand the full impact until Elvis told me what had happened nearly two and a half years later in Las Vegas!

During the early minutes of the performance as Elvis finished singing, "Why Me, Lord?", he placed his microphone on the stand, lowered his head in frustration and turned toward me with tears coursing down his reddened cheeks.

While he unsuccessfully restrained his emotions, he appeared to be asking, *"Why are you here? Where do I turn? Yet, I know, and I'm not sure I want to."*

What seemed like an eternity passed before he broke his intense gaze, determinedly jerked the microphone off its pedestal, and returned to the audience to sing the song for a second time.

Fulfilling the last of the suggestions, my pastor had made concerning Elvis' possible reactions during the concert, he walked to the corner of the stage nearest to me.

With a quizzical expression he grinned, made a frown, and replaced it with a smile by a wave of his hand before curiously asking, "Why the long face?"

My answer was too long and complicated, so I simply lowered my head and remained silent. At least he realized that I wasn't there to merely watch the show. He had sensed Someone larger than both of us, and that was a tremendous step in the right direction.

4

PRAYING IN THE CHAPEL

"It's their move next," the Lord reminded me in the weeks following his concert, "part of the group that travels with Elvis will be in the area and I want you to go see them."

The night of their appearance, Jerry and I were in the audience. Hal walked on stage and stood looking at me as if he'd seen a ghost. His obvious curiosity soon brought an outward reaction. "How many of you have seen us before?" he asked. Several hands were raised in response to that and two other questions. The fourth was more direct as Hal looked at me and requested, "How many of you saw us with Elvis in June?"

As I slowly raised my hand, Hal nodded satisfactorily and replied, "Yes, that's *just* what I thought!"

After the concert ended I asked the Lord to send Hal to talk to me this time. After all, I had made the first move at Elvis' concert and I didn't want them to think my reasons were anything but spiritual.

However, by the time Jerry and I left our seats, Hal had already walked away from the area.

As I stepped down from the bleachers, I glanced back just in time to see Hal running past people calling to him as he hurried over to us.

I stifled a smile and stopped to wait on him. He came to a breathless stop in front of us as I reached out to shake his hand, asking, "Do you remember me?"

"Why, sure, I do," he responded in an offended tone. "Why would you have to ask something like that? Why do you think I was staring at you all through the show?"

Leaving his questions unanswered I continued, "I'm still

praying for Elvis. And I won't quit, either! Oh . . . I added your name to the list, too."

"You what?" Hal replied with a startled glance.

"I'm still praying for Elvis," I repeated, "and I'm praying for you, too."

"Wait right here a minute," Hal said in a demanding voice. "I have to run an errand, but I want to talk to you some more before you leave."

"Leave now, you've said enough," the Lord whispered as Hal walked away.

I had been analyzing Elvis' life and I wondered why I'd felt a hesitancy from him during the concert. I found myself trying to decide if he too might be trying to escape something God wanted him to do.

As I considered these things the Lord inquired in a thought-provoking manner, "Do you think Elvis might have been called to be an evangelist?"

"No," I bluntly replied. "Maybe a gospel singer. But a preacher? There's no way!"

However, the longer I considered the Lord's statement, the more logical it became.

My suspicion mounted until I phoned one of Elvis' friends in Tupelo for another opinion.

"Could Elvis have been called into the ministry years ago?" I cautiously asked.

"Well, let me put it this way. There are preachers in the family. Several of them. Let's just leave it at that," she said with a smile I could feel all the way from Mississippi.

I hung up the receiver knowing I had enough evidence to be reasonably sure, and during the next few months I gathered enough to convict him in any court!

During the fall, rumors linking Elvis with evangelism began appearing in various places.

One national publication stated openly that evangelism would be a perfect outlet for Elvis, giving him greater victories with more self-satisfaction than he'd ever known before.

Still another source suggested that Elvis would probably quit show business for the ministry. They reported that he was beginning to seriously consider changing to Gospel singing and evangelism.

At least someone was placing things where Elvis could hear them.

Throughout the following weeks the Lord confirmed and reconfirmed that I was to continue praying. I became aware that in order to reach Elvis I would have to be able to yield to the Lord to the point of literally telling him his own life story.

Feeling led to stop by the church to pray one afternoon, I knelt and began petitioning God for Elvis' soul. As I continued I felt a hand on my right arm as if I was to stand up. "Let's go," the Lord boldly stated.

"Go where?" I asked, looking around to see if He was actually visible.

"To Memphis!" He exclaimed.

I considered the answer that I'd been waiting on for the past year. "Okay. When?" I inquired.

"Soon," was His final reply. "Very soon."

In December of 1974, Elvis cancelled all professional plans due to ill health. That sickness culminated in a three-week hospital stay during January, 1975.

The Blackwood Brothers Quartet, a group that Elvis nearly joined before his Sun Studio days, were in our area.

I wanted to ask James to pray for Elvis, but to assure me that the Lord didn't mind if we talked, I asked Him to lead James into a specific hallway at a specific time. As I rounded the corner, my answer was plain, because there was James walking solitarily down the hall.

I greeted him and tried to cram nearly two years of details into five minutes. After I rambled on incoherently about Elvis' reactions and the concert, I gave him a copy of a letter I'd sent to Pat Robertson, expressing the same things about Elvis that I'd tried to explain to him, asked for his help through prayer and left.

The next few months were occupied by days filled with prayer, waiting, and sleepless nights. My constant request was for the Lord to lead people to Elvis to witness to him, or talk to him personally. I know that request was granted many times.

I'd begun to settle down in the routine of waiting for Elvis to come back to Kansas City again. I could have seen him any number of times around the country, but God didn't send me, so I didn't go.

Unexpectedly, one day in June, the Lord stopped me in my tracks by casually asking, "Are you going to Memphis for Labor Day weekend?"

"There's really no reason to go," I immediately replied while

I tried to recall what we could do in Memphis besides see Elvis. "Anyway, Elvis will be in Las Vegas, so why should we go to Memphis? He'll be at the Hilton!"

"No, he won't be in Las Vegas," He stated emphatically. "He'll be in Memphis at Baptist Memorial Hospital. I'm going to allow him to stay in Las Vegas a couple of days and then I'll send him home to Memphis."

I meditated upon His overwhelming certainty and waited for further developments.

The Lord was dealing with me to begin fasting. I sensed it would be a *long* one this time, so I hesitated. Each day it became more obvious that the inevitable was approaching.

"Start a three-week fast . . . now," the Lord requested.

"Now?" I questioned, not believing the timing. I was in the midst of preparing a large meal for guests, my favorite meal! "Can't it wait until morning?" I pleaded.

There was no answer, so I assumed He didn't mind.

After I'd feasted on what I knew would seem like my last meal at times, I began having a guilt complex! I realized I had time to attend church if I hurried, so sacrificing an evening with friends I went, hoping it would stay my penalty for disobedience.

Two blocks from the sanctuary I began having severe stomach pains. I prayed, rebuked, and pleaded but they remained. It was obvious that I couldn't go to church in this shape, so I drove to the gas station to fill up the car in order to stall for time.

While I was there I slipped into the restroom and immediately lost the meal I had consumed, along with everything else I'd eaten that day.

After I decided I'd probably live, I walked out to the car. As I closed the door, the Lord matter-of-factly stated, "Now, start your fast."

Without any hesitation I obeyed!

On the first day of the fast I was shown a white-hooded creature that was promptly introduced as "death."

"Lord, what are You trying to tell me?" I reservedly asked.

"Elvis' life will be endangered before you will have the opportunity to reach him," was His steady reply.

The days continued to pass as so many numbers on a calendar until the third week of the fast when I received a second vision that almost seemed ridiculous in nature.

As I knelt in prayer I suddenly found myself in a strange and distant city: obviously Las Vegas. Through thick darkness

I struggled down a crowded street lined with flashing neon lights. I began asking people where the Las Vegas Hilton was located. Those going in the opposite direction shoved me aside, then after walking several blocks, someone eventually answered by pointing in a specific direction saying, "It's one-half mile that way. But you're not out here alone are you?"

"Yes," I muttered as I glanced around bewildered as to how I got here in the first place. I walked alone in complete darkness until the neon lights were well behind me before I saw the Hilton. As I approached it, I saw a pair of black iron gates prohibiting entry to the front circle drive. I began binding all the forces keeping me out and the gates swung open. I didn't walk through because it wasn't time yet.

The following day the words "Isaiah 45" kept echoing through my mind until I eventually gave in to the urging and opened my Bible to the suggested passage. The first two Scriptures were enough to convince me that the vision had merit.

The vision was explained as I read, "Thus saith the Lord . . . I will loose the loins of kings, to open before him the two leaved gates; and the gates shall not be shut. I will go before thee, and make the crooked places straight . . ." (Isa. 45:1-2).

The final week of August, 1975, brought with it the Las Vegas Hilton engagement the Lord had warned me about. I immediately began watching for news releases concerning Elvis. After the first two days he left Vegas and entered Baptist Memorial Hospital in Memphis as previously prescribed.

The Lord had been silent concerning Memphis after the suggestions about going on Labor Day weekend. Needing further proof, I asked the Lord to allow Jerry to suggest leaving for Memphis at noon on Friday, because he knew nothing about any preparatory guidance.

That evening after dinner, Jerry abruptly looked across the room casually suggesting, "Let's go to Memphis this weekend. I've already checked and I can get off at noon Friday. While we're there you can pray for Elvis at the hospital."

I shared my prayer request with him and began planning to go.

Before Friday I grappled with my decision based on rationality! Indecision resulted, so I talked with Warren Black, Regional Director of the 700 Club. During our conversation I asked, "How far does faith go? Does it get up and drive 500 miles to pray for someone that you don't stand a chance to talk to without God's direct intervention?"

"Sit down and analyze your thoughts," Warren advised, "after you've eliminated the doubts and worries, if you find peace, then you know you're to go."

Later that night I did as he suggested and became even more sure that I should go. But I wanted the Lord to confirm my decision again. Around morning the Lord awakened me, and in a vision I saw Him standing to my left, handing me a shepherd's staff. Realizing that this was used as a symbol of authority throughout the Scriptures I managed to ask through my tears, "Does this mean I am to go?"

"Yes . . . go," came His peaceful reply.

Saturday morning I walked into Baptist Memorial Hospital in Memphis and asked the receptionist at the main desk if there was a chapel in the hospital. I'd heard Elvis was on the eighteenth floor.

"Yes, one on every floor," she proudly exclaimed.

Well, that was about eighteen floors closer to Elvis than I thought I'd get. Then as I stepped onto the elevator, pleased with my ability to get at least that close and pray, a nurse grabbed me urgently requesting, "Look, quick! There's Elvis' doctor! He must be going up to check on him."

"Oh, is Elvis still here?" I asked through my amusement at the way the Lord was allowing things to fall into place . . . again.

"Oh, yes, he's still here," she knowingly replied.

"It's been over a week since he was admitted, hasn't it?" I inquired. "Have they found out what was wrong yet?"

"Well, some of the things," she added authoritatively, "he has problems with his liver, his blood pressure, and his colon is acting up again."

Now I had a complete medical report to pray about.

Two nurses directed me to the chapel, one of them was named Thornton, the other Marian! Another coincidence!

As I stepped inside the chapel the pages of a Bible fluttered open to Ecclesiastes 8:1-10. I read the passage and understood the more than obvious meaning. Then for over two hours I interceded in the Spirit for Elvis' health and soul before the Lord released me to leave the room.

When I walked into the main lobby again, Jerry gasped, "Where have you been?"

"Praying. Why?" I asked.

"You look like you've been in a battle!" he exclaimed.

"I have been," I repeated in a revealing tone, "I have been."

Later at Graceland, Elvis' home, I talked with a girl from England and one from France, who had come over for Elvis' Vegas shows. When he became suddenly ill they followed him to Memphis.

"How did Elvis sound in Vegas?" I asked.

"The orchestra had to almost totally undergird him and the backup singers had to fill in for the notes he couldn't hit. It was terrible. I felt so sorry for him," one of the girls sympathetically remarked.

Jerry and I attended First Assembly of God in Memphis the next morning. As we parked next to a silver Cadillac Seville, Jerry teasingly remarked, "Think this could be one of Elvis' boys' cars?"

"Somehow, I doubt it!" I laughingly replied.

Inside the sanctuary a black-haired boy walked by us repeatedly, speaking each time he passed. He seemed to be acting strange, but I thought it was probably just me.

After services we drove to the river. As I walked through the park a hobo approached me asking for money. Before I had time to consider granting his request the power of the Spirit came upon me and I began quoting, ". . . Silver and gold have I none, but such as I have give I unto thee. . . ."

While he stood amazed and emotionally moved, I continued spontaneously quoting other Scriptures pertaining to salvation.

Before I left the park, he knelt and accepted Jesus Christ as his Saviour.

It didn't seem to matter where I went during the time I prayed for Elvis, the Lord always had someone such as this man for me to pray with for His glory. The choice to help them was totally mine.

It was as if He was saying, "Will you stoop this *low* to reach that *high?*" The answer was always a firm "Yes," because I didn't look at them with the eyes of the world. Had my answer been negative, I'm sure I'd never have reached Elvis.

Tupelo, Mississippi, Elvis' birthplace, was our next destination. I wanted to meet the lady I'd been calling during the past two years. I thought I'd already fulfilled my obligation at the hospital, but the further away from Memphis we drove, the more restless I became.

"It's no use. I can't go on," I told Jerry shaking my head

in bewilderment. "Let's go back to Memphis."

We pulled up in front of Elvis' house just as the black-haired boy in the silver Seville from church drove to the front gates. Jerry and I looked at each other, then toward him as he smiled and waved before turning toward the hospital.

The Lord took that as a cue and added, "Go back and pray again."

That's why I couldn't go to Tupelo, there was more work to do, along with some confirming.

So it was back to the eighteenth floor. But this time when the elevator doors opened the black-haired boy was leaning against the opposite wall. He and I exchanged satisfied looks, he grinned and took off in the direction of Elvis' room.

The Lord's presence was in the chapel when I walked in to pray for another two hours. This time before I left He told me to read the Twentieth Psalm. It was apparent that He had answered my requests, but it was difficult to leave that floor knowing that if I could only talk to Elvis *all* my requests might be fulfilled that day.

On the way down in the elevator I used the time to ask the Lord why I had to drive a thousand miles for no more visible results than I'd received.

"It was time to let Elvis see just how determined you are. He knew you were here," He answered.

At six o'clock on Monday morning the Lord awakened me saying, "Get up and start watching for the Blackwood Brothers' bus."

We were in the wrong part of town to see them or their bus! But, I began watching anyway. Later, as we left the motel, I had given up on seeing anything. Just as I glanced toward the intersection, there it sat!

"Follow that bus," I told Jerry while I kept a fixed gaze on the vehicle to insure its reality.

We followed Jimmy home, and as he stepped down from the bus I asked, "Do you want to do a little witnessing?"

"Well, I've been driving all night," he sighed, "but what did you have in mind?"

"It's Elvis, Jimmy . . . he's in the hospital again and someone needs to help him," I related.

"I'll be praying, but call Cecil, too," he suggested.

After Jimmy, his wife, and I prayed for Elvis, I phoned Cecil and explained the need to him. He, too, offered prayers and slowly added, "Are you the one who gave James that letter?"

"Yes . . . it was me," I replied.

As we closed our conversation, Cecil again assured me that he would pray.

On our way back to Graceland to ask how Elvis was, a radio station reported Elvis' condition was improving and concluded by playing his rendition of "He Touched Me." I smiled, knowing beyond any speculation that He definitely had.

"When will Elvis be home?" I asked his Uncle Vester.

"They're saying he'll be out in a few days. He's beginning to get better," he replied.

The need to remain in Memphis left as he had answered, and I came home assured that God's will had been done.

Why all the caution when approaching Elvis? To begin with, God was leading and opening the doors. He had started me on this journey and He would complete it, not me. And no one walked into Elvis' world uninvited.

Incidentally, that was exactly four years to the day I'd asked Mike McGregor to tell Elvis that I'd be back again! I had been back, but what a change in me!

5

HE ADDED A TEAR

I had been delegated to obtain advertising posters and personalized 700 Club advertisement papers for a witnessing project in our community.

When I phoned Warren Black at his office to request the necessary amount, he surprised me by offering, "Let me know the day before you come, and you can counsel during the 700 Club program."

That was something I had wanted to do since the program first aired in Kansas City. As I hung the receiver on the hook I asked, "Lord, what day should I go?"

"Tuesday," came His immediate reply.

That evening as I related the events to Jerry he looked at me in amusement, realizing the odds of my being involved in receiving a simple uncomplicated invitation to anything! "The way your luck runs, that man we were told has Elvis in the number one position on his prayer list will be interviewed that day."

I ignored his teasing until the evening paper arrived listing the following week's schedule of 700 Club guests. Jerry's intuition was right! Listed beside Tuesday was the name he had suggested.

During the course of the speaker's presentation that Tuesday came a report of a proposed service to be held in Madison Square Garden in New York. Elvis was to be there to sing Gospel songs before and after this man's speaking, and, hopefully, Elvis wouldn't be able to stand the pressure and he'd repent.

I came home elated over the possibilities of my prayers being answered and the job being finished.

The program was re-shown again late Saturday night. As

I watched my earlier enthusiasm began subsiding. The motives and the way it was to be done didn't seem to be like the Lord at all. But how could this possibly be?

Toward the early morning hours after I'd paced the floor and prayed all night the Lord spoke to me as plain as I've ever heard Him, saying, "Read Proverbs 29:11 and you'll understand."

After analyzing the Scripture I prayed, "Lord, I'll accept what You've shown me. But I want to talk to the man in question before I can believe all of this. But could You arrange it for about three in the morning when he's 'run down' some?"

The Lord answered that request quickly. Within a few weeks I began seeing posters announcing his arrival in Kansas City for a series of New Year's Eve services.

On the appointed day, a friend of mine named Denise, and I drove to the auditorium where he was scheduled to speak. After we had discovered he hadn't arrived yet, the Lord directed us to the pastor of the local Assembly of God Church.

As I walked into his office, he pulled the telephone receiver away from his ear and asked, "Can I do something for you?"

"Yes, I'm Mary Ann Thornton, and I want to talk to you briefly about Elvis and the man that's scheduled to speak in town tonight."

"Just a minute," he replied, returning to his call with a slight smile. After ending the conversation he turned to me saying, "When you walked in I was talking about tonight's meeting. Now what can I do for you?"

As I sat down in a chair I explained, "The Lord has been leading me for several months concerning Elvis' soul. I understand the evangelist that is scheduled to speak tonight is interested in Elvis, too. I want to share with him and if it's the Lord's will he can use what's helpful in order to get the job done. Could you possibly arrange a meeting for me?"

"Yes, I'll try to set up an appointment with him," the pastor replied nervously. Glancing toward me he apologetically suggested, "Due to the late meetings, would three in the morning be acceptable?"

"Perfect," I remarked satisfactorily, as I reflected on my previous request for this exact time.

Elvis was scheduled to perform in a New Year's Eve concert in Pontiac, Michigan, that night. At least the evangelist and I could encourage each other by praying together for him. That alone would make the trip worthwhile.

In order to make the evening 100 percent productive and involve Elvis as well as the speaker and me, I asked the Lord to illustrate openly if Elvis was being reached when I prayed by allowing something unusual to occur during the performance. Preferably something that would require Elvis' undivided attention and yet would be important enough that I'd hear about it afterwards.

The distinct impression that he would rip the seat out of his jumpsuit entered my mind. "Oh Lord, you wouldn't allow that!" I replied vocally to my thoughts, as one of Elvis' standing jokes about his clothes ripping during the concerts came to my mind.

Around midnight, when Denise and I arrived at the auditorium, I located the pastor of the Assembly of God Church. "Did you manage to set up the appointment? What did he say?" I questioned.

"Yes, and he *definitely* wants to talk to you after the last service tonight. He'll wait for you beside the stage door," was his enthusiastic reply.

Throughout the entire meeting the evangelist kept looking toward me in much the same way that Elvis and Hal had, although he didn't know who I was yet.

After the conclusion of the service the minister walked out the stage door. As I hurried to him I glanced at my watch. It was 3 A.M. "I'm Mary Ann," I assured him while reaching to shake his hand. "The one the pastor told you about." As his facial expression began to pale, I inquired, "Don't you remember?"

"Yeah, I remember," he gruffly answered, "but I'm too tired to talk about anything now!"

"Let's pray then and the Lord will strengthen you," I quickly suggested, not believing what I was seeing or hearing.

"If you want to pray for something, pray for this meetin' they had here tonight! Call me at my office some time and tell me about this thing with Elvis!" he bitterly responded, walking away with a grumble.

It was obvious that he didn't want to talk, but if he only knew, I would have gladly shared anything I knew and helped him to reach Elvis.

Sadly, Proverbs 29:11 became even more clear to me.

On New Year's Day a wire photo of Elvis from the previous night's concert appeared in the paper, illustrating to everyone just how sick he was.

The following morning an article with the unmistakable heading, "Gyrating Pelvis too Much for Pants," explained that Elvis' jumpsuit had ripped after he'd begun his concert! Proving that my impression had been genuine.

The next Sunday during altar service, the Lord broke the stillness that had reigned for the past few weeks by showing me a vision of Himself standing in front of a golden throne with a beautifully ornate crown in His hands. As He walked toward me to lay it down, the effect of His presence was visible upon the people kneeling around me and they began weeping or trembling.

After placing the crown beside me, He brought a sceptre that had been laying beside the throne and laid it down. His actions told me that He was illustrating to me that I possessed His authority, as well as His salvation.

"Arise and go in the power of the Spirit," He softly instructed.

Turning to my pastor who had joined us at the altar, I pleaded, "But I don't know *where* He wants me to go!"

Again the Lord repeated His firm but gentle command.

"Where does He want me to go, Pastor," I again requested.

"That's not for you to worry about," he assured me. "He will tell you where you are to go."

While he comforted me, the Lord, for the third time, restated His simple request.

My impatience began showing again as I fell prey to one of Satan's oldest tricks to destroy faith.

"Take Elvis back, Lord," I said in a defeated attitude. "I'm tired. There's so many others that could do the job easier and better than me. I wanted to help, but I can't seem to reach him."

He chose this moment to talk to me about this, too.

"If you think your patience is being tried, consider Mine," the Lord began methodically explaining in answer to my ill-chosen request. "For years I've watched my people being persecuted and martyred while they prayed for My soon return. Yet I have patience and trust the Father throughout it all."

As He finished speaking He revealed Himself to me with His face mutilated and blood dripping down His cheeks from a crown of thorns cutting into His forehead.

As that faded I saw Him in a way I understood from studying the description recorded in Revelation 1, with His hair white as wool, depicting fatherhood, while His eyes were as a flame of fire, illustrating His all-penetrating intelligence. The message

40

that followed was, *"You can't win a crown unless you bear a cross."* I silenced my murmuring once again and resumed my praying.

To enforce His message even more, the Lord added a dream in which I was seated alone in a large auditorium. As Elvis walked onto the stage to perform, I immediately opened my mouth to start talking to him about the Lord, but before I could proceed Elvis picked up the microphone, looked at me, and suggested, "Read James 5:10."

At daybreak, when I recalled the dream, I fell out of bed charging through the house to get my Bible. I was less than jubilant over the message that read, "Take, my brethren, the prophets, who have spoken in the name of the Lord, for an example of suffering affliction, and of patience."

I grasped the obvious meaning, along with the other messages I'd received over the past week and understood that it wasn't time to approach Elvis yet, regardless of how impatient I might become. Inwardly, I didn't want to contact him until he was ready to talk, but feelings of the moment tend to disrupt our lives.

After my motives were rearranged again, I received a series of three identical dreams on three consecutive nights.

In each of them I'd been turning the pages of a newspaper until I located an announcement of an appearance by Elvis in Kansas City.

On the day of the third dream, I phoned Jan, a friend, requesting, "Pray with me about Elvis today. If I'm to sit back and pray behind the scenes and never talk to him personally, then I have to know so I won't set my goals too high. It looks like the Lord wants me to carry through to the end. But I have to be positive. Will you help me to pray?"

"I'll do better than that," she replied. "Benita and I will come over and pray with you right now."

Within thirty minutes they had arrived and we had begun praying.

Each of us began quietly petitioning the Lord. I knew I needed some totally irreversible proof concerning Elvis. But since Jan and Benita were both sympathetic to my burden, that ruled out a lot of things I could ask for, because Satan would be able to rob me of anything our intellects were involved in.

However, I knew Jan had been allowed to see the Lord on various occasions, so I began to ask Him to confirm whether I'd

41

reach Elvis or not by allowing Jan to see Him standing to my left, slightly bent over me, and holding a shepherd's crook over my head. That should be sufficient for me and vague enough that she would be impartial with her response.

After several minutes of waiting, Jan quizzically stated, "Mary Ann, I have something to tell you. Except I don't know if it will make any sense at all."

"What is it Jan?" I replied expectantly, sighing with relief.

"Well, it's the Lord, Mary Ann. And He's standing to your left, slightly bent over you, and He's holding a shepherd's crook over your head . . . and there's a tear in His eye." Jan answered in a confused tone.

I immediately shared my request with her. Jan understood then, but we all wondered exactly why He had added the tear.

Within a few days another vision was granted picturing Denise and I in a car north of Elvis' home, Graceland, preparing to turn south onto Elvis Presley Boulevard. As I watched, I saw trees engulfed in flames, but not consumed, in a field northwest of the mansion. A large crowd had gathered at the gates and there were people announcing news bulletins.

"Something's happened to Elvis, we've got to get down there," I hurriedly remarked to her as we turned south toward the house.

Then came a pause in the vision.

As it began again, I was standing alone in a hall looking at an Exit sign above a stairway. I slowly walked down a half flight of stairs and turned left to complete the descent to a lower hall. I walked through the first doorway on the right and entered the second door on my left. It ended in an abrupt halt when I looked up and saw Elvis sitting at a game table waiting for me.

From January onward I had sensed Elvis would be back before summer. On April twenty-first his concert at Kemper Arena in Kansas City was announced! That confirmed the three dreams of newspaper announcements that I'd received several weeks earlier.

During the first ten hours of ticket sales all 18,000 seats were sold. As Jan and I waited in line to buy our tickets, we heard people talking about Elvis' failing health. Everyone seemed very concerned.

"Now, Lord, we need to get the people at church praying for Elvis without my having to ask them," I decided one day when I was plotting to locate prayer support for the upcoming concert.

42

He answered during church services when an evangelist abruptly switched the topic of his sermon to what an effect Elvis could have if he surrendered to God's will. Then, to my delight, he proceeded to challenge everyone there to go home and get on their knees and pray for Elvis' soul!

It had been thirty-two months of praying now! I was beginning to compare reaching Elvis to scaling Mount Everest! But this was no time to quit.

6

COME BEFORE WINTER

The three weeks between ticket sales and Elvis' concert passed rapidly.

I contacted Hal's office in Nashville, two days before Elvis' arrival in Kansas City on April twenty-first, and left a message telling him I'd be in the Holiday Inn Coffee Shoppe between one-thirty and two o'clock on the afternoon of the concert, if he wanted to talk to me about Elvis, he could contact me there.

Hal was out of the office at the time so I left a note for him hoping it would be delivered.

Later, I learned from another member of the group that he'd come running into rehearsal that night exclaiming, "Mary Ann called . . . something's up!"

That Sunday night a conversation radiating from the heavens awakened me. It was between God and Satan regarding Elvis' soul.

I listened as Satan threw angry accusations with a screeching hateful voice. The Lord repeatedly answered him as an adult would a temperamental child by calmly stating, "But you *know* you can't have his soul!"

After the conversation changed sides several times, my ears were closed to the commotion and I drifted into a peaceful sleep knowing that the battle was the Lord's.

The following day, during my normal routines, the Lord interrupted me by adding this bit of information about Elvis' state of mind, "He is in deep despair and pain, and he's searching, searching, searching. But he shall find it. Write down what I have told you and place it in your Bible."

I did as He suggested and considered the words, realizing that only God could know the meditations of a person's heart.

The day for the concert arrived. As I awakened, the Lord began saying, "One year . . . he has one year."

"What are you saying?" I inquired. "I'll need a Scripture to back up whatever it is You are leading up to."

"Open your Bible," came the brief reply.

I picked up my study Bible and opened it to Isaiah 21. The first thing my eyes fell upon was in verse 16 stating, "For thus hath the Lord said unto me, Within a year . . . all the glory . . . shall fall." I quickly closed the Bible with a new premonition concerning the future.

Jan and I went to the Holiday Inn Coffee Shoppe to eat lunch and wait for Hal. After we had been seated for a few minutes, Jan looked slowly across the booth saying, "The Lord is impressing me that you will be paged soon."

Less than five minutes had passed before my name was called over the hotel speaker system. I waited for a repetition before I asked the cashier where the house phones were located.

As I followed her directions, they led me into the lobby and I realized these were the same phones the Lord had spoken to me about nearly two years earlier. I had been paged to them after all!

"Yes," I answered cautiously as I picked up the receiver.

"Mary? This is Hal. What do you want to talk about?" he asked.

"The Lord . . . and Elvis," I explained, realizing he had reversed my message stating "if *he* wanted to talk."

After I answered, Hal quickly placed his hand over the receiver and asked someone else in the room several questions. After the replies were made, Hal returned to the phone relating, "Okay, come on over. It's all right. We're on the sixth floor of the Hilton Inn."

"Where is that?" I inquired. I didn't even know there was a Hilton in Kansas City!

"Near the freeway," he replied.

"Can't you be more specific?" I reasoned. "Everything is near a freeway!"

"I can see the airport by the river. Does that help any?" he asked.

"Yes, that helps. I know where that is," I answered.

"How long will it take you to get here, so we'll know how long to hold your names on the security list?" he inquired.

"Expect me in five minutes," I exclaimed. "But give me an hour! I may get lost and have to go home and start over again!"

"Okay, we'll wait for you," Hal laughed.

Jan and I hurried out of the Holiday Inn after paying double for our lunches. We didn't have time to wait for change!

Once in the car I realized I needed to ask someone for some directions, so I picked up the microphone on my CB radio and without any preliminaries asked, "Does *anyone* know how to get to the Hilton Inn?"

"Where are you now?" came the immediate reply. "That's where I'm going too. If you'll tell me what kind of car you're driving I'll lead you right to it."

As Jan and I looked at each other in amazement at the way God was providing, I told him what type of automobile we were driving and where we were located.

"Okay, I'm just ahead of you. I'll stop and wait. I'm driving a Monte Carlo, watch for me. When I turn a corner on the way, I'll pull over and wait for you there before I proceed," he replied.

After we arrived at the hotel I thanked the man for his help and went to the registration desk, as Hal had advised.

"We were told to have our names verified here for the sixth floor security clearance," I informed the desk clerk.

"Just a minute," was her doubtful reply, "I'll have to talk to someone else first."

The manager appeared from his office curiously asking, "Well, what can I do for you girls today?"

"We're expected on the floor Elvis has reserved, the sixth floor," I said. "I was to have you call upstairs and ask for Hal. He'll verify our expected presence. Our names are on the security list."

After suspiciously dialing the sixth floor, he turned with a quizzical expression and said, "You're expected. Go on up, the elevators are on your left."

As the elevator doors opened on the top floor, we were greeted by several security guards sitting around a table holding a list of names.

I immediately told them who we were and they quickly found our names on the list directly under Vernon, Elvis' Dad's name.

"Go to your left for Hal's room. You girls belong up here," they remarked.

I turned to walk down the hall . . . another hall . . . just like

Baptist Memorial Hospital, after looking wistfully at the double doors of Elvis' suite and restraining an urge to throw the door open and get it over with!

Getting past the security was extremely simple, which isn't usually the case, or so I understand. Plus, anyone who knows anything about Elvis, knows you didn't simply stroll onto the floor he was staying on without so much as being searched.

Before Jan and I had walked more than four feet the elevator opened again and a girl stepped off asking, "Did anyone of you see a brown-headed girl get off here? She's my friend and I can't find her anyplace."

Before she'd had time to finish her question four or five of the guards were standing up with their hands on their guns requesting, "Maybe you'd like for us to escort you downstairs to find her . . . and a ride to the police station."

She grew pale and backed onto the elevator without another word.

Before the day was over I saw that scene repeated several times. Each time, I praised the Lord that He had put a calmness in the hearts of the people who allowed us up there.

Hal met us in the hall and continued to walk with us to his room. As soon as we were seated, he sat down on the floor in front of me and stated very seriously, "I feel like I can talk to you, I don't know why, but I have that impression. And I've got a lot of problems I need to talk about. I'm about ready to give up trying."

Then for over five hours he proceeded to pour out his doubts, fears, and anxieties. And, as is His normal way, the Lord ministered to him by giving me the words of comfort and encouragement for him.

Eventually, speaking of Elvis, Hal interjected some of the things that Elvis had talked to him about during the long nights on tours.

However, he unsuccessfully kept trying to convince me that Elvis was in perfect health, when all anyone had to do was look at him to see differently . . . much less the fact that the Lord had been keeping me informed otherwise.

I shared my intentions as far as Elvis' life was concerned. I didn't want any misunderstandings.

Several invitations were extended for Elvis' next engagement in Lake Tahoe, Nevada, which was to begin a few days after the present ten-city tour ended. One of the invitations was complete with private jet service, a room, my own body-guard (in case I

47

didn't trust them), plus all the time I could possibly want to talk to and pray with Elvis.

Sounded like what I'd been waiting for, right? Wrong! No Spirit witness accompanied the invitations, and there had been no previous guidance to even vaguely suggest a trip to Lake Tahoe.

When I declined those offers to Tahoe they were quickly replaced by standing invitations to his Las Vegas appearances.

"We'll see, but the way Elvis has been leaving Vegas, I'm afraid I'd get out there and he'd be in Memphis at Baptist Memorial!" I told Hal. "Besides, if God even allows you in Las Vegas again it'll be the last time, and it will be because He wants something accomplished."

"Listen, all we really want is for Elvis to use his talent for God's glory," Jan remarked.

"No," I disagreed, "I think there's a lot more to it than that. I think Elvis is called to be an evangelist. That's what the Lord wants now and that's what he should be doing now."

While I held my breath, awaiting Hal's reaction, he answered without so much as raising his head, "Yep, Elvis is a preacher all right! He preaches all night sometimes, to anyone who will listen to him. If no one else will, then I listen. More than one person has walked out on Elvis during the night because they didn't want to hear his 'Jesus stuff.' I've heard a lot of good preachers in my time, but Elvis sure knows the Word."

My guidance had been correct, I thought as I took a deep breath, just as Hal picked up my Bible and pulled out the note about Elvis' searching and despair. After reading it he asked, "What's this all about?"

"Oh, just something the Lord told me yesterday concerning Elvis," I casually replied.

"That's not exactly what I've been telling you all afternoon, is it?" Hal nervously responded.

"No," I answered, while Hal rubbed his forehead and walked the floor allowing his true feelings to come tumbling out in a torrent of explanations about Elvis' fear of dying young like his mother and an uncle.

After a spell of pacing the floor, he turned abruptly and looked out the window at a signboard in front of the hotel that read: Welcome 700 Club Prayer Partners. "What is this?" he angrily demanded.

I stifled a grin, adding, "Oh that! Wasn't that nice of the Lord? I noticed it when I came in."

After several hours of down-to-earth discussion about Elvis, along with the instructions, *"Don't* act impressed when you *do* meet him! That's very important," I assured Hal that I could handle Elvis because I knew him as well as I knew myself.

Around seven o'clock I went to the lobby to locate Jan, who had come down earlier. I walked into a restaurant to find her and found Charley Hodge, a backup guitar player for Elvis, Jackie Kahane, the show's comedian, Bill Baize, who sang tenor for the Stamps Quartet at one time, and several others who travelled with Elvis regularly.

I ultimately had Jan paged. While waiting at the registration desk, a man that had been standing by the restaurant door walked over to me asking, "Who are you looking for?"

"Jan," I reluctantly answered.

"Oh! She's out beside your car waiting for you," he answered, in a tone illustrating how simple the answer was, while pointing to my car.

I walked out puzzled as to how he knew Jan without any descriptions, which car was mine, where it was parked, or basically, why he was so ready to assist me. I hadn't told anyone the things he knew. So it was apparent that someone had been checking.

While we drove to Kemper I recalled that this man was the one everyone referred to as the buffer between Elvis and everyone else.

After we arrived, Jan and I quickly found our seats. Instead of being in front of Elvis I was behind him again! It didn't matter, we had asked the Lord to put us where He wanted us, even if it *was* seventeen rows into the second balcony!

During intermission, we left our seats and missed most of Elvis' first song before we could return.

As I walked carefully down the aisle to avoid stumbling in the dark, I stopped and looked toward the stage after his singing came to an abrupt halt. Elvis had turned around and was looking up at me. I stopped my descent and waited. I tried to shrug off his actions as a standard move, but I knew otherwise. We exchanged intense looks for several minutes, much like throughout the concert twenty-one months earlier.

Again, I found myself wondering what he kept seeing. Besides that, I was above *and* behind him. And, how does he know when I walk into a totally dark auditorium? Elvis was even near-sighted! And yet he *still* turned around and recognized me. This was one mystery I wanted solved!

During the concert Elvis continued turning and made several inuendos concerning "someone coming back to the Hilton to talk after the show."

Hal had asked that I come back to the hotel after the concert so he could check with the tour management to see if they'd loosen security so I could meet Elvis. After a refusal, Elvis dropped into one of his varied moods and went to bed. So we settled for an exchange of messages.

I had considered this episode closed until the Lord began impressing me to leave a message for Elvis from Him. I had no idea what it was, but as I sat there the words began to form a thought pattern, and the more clear it became, the more certain I was that this was one message I didn't want to deliver!

I looked at Hal knowing how he had been watching the disturbed expression on my face. I hesitated and the Lord again affirmed His message without demanding that I deliver it. His only reminder was, "But you know you should say it."

I nodded slowly in silent acceptance of the words He had been speaking.

Slowly, I began to gather enough strength and breath to enable me to repeat the message.

"Tell Elvis . . . tell him that I came here in God's love . . . and in His will. But you tell him this, because I can't. You see, he can't or doesn't want to talk to me tonight. It's not *from* me. It's from the Lord. 'Elvis has one year to live . . . after that he'll die'." I slowly related. "Man, I won't be near him when it happens and God won't kill him. God doesn't kill anyone," I abruptly explained as Hal watched in unbelief. "It's a warning. Tell him he'd better run. Just tell Elvis to run . . . fast. He's going to have to turn it *all* over to the Lord. Warn him. Just *please* warn him."

I sat trembling as I wept uncontrollably listening to Hal make a nervous threat about my welfare.

On the way to the elevator, Hal encouraged me to stay out of trouble.

"Just tell Elvis," I pleaded as the doors slid shut.

On the way home as I rehearsed the evening's activities I recalled the Lord's remark concerning one year and the confirming Scripture in Isaiah 21:16.

Although there was a feeling of doom in the air now, I knew that Elvis would be reached somehow.

Hal and I crossed paths again eight months and 1,400 miles

later. But in the meantime, I pondered the strange message I'd been asked to deliver. I asked, "Why"? more times than I can count. And each time the Lord assured me that Elvis was being warned of impending disaster. It wasn't cruel as I had first thought. Instead, it was mercy extended in the form of words.

Soon the Lord began preparing me through more visions, dreams, and Scriptures, that came from praying.

In the first dream I received after the concert, I was standing at a hotel registration desk with suitcase in hand! Sighing heavily and then in a monotonous tone I said, "Well, this is the third time now!"

I really thought that one over! I'd only seen Elvis twice in local concerts since the Lord had asked me to pray for him, but here I'd had luggage. It appeared that the price of seeing Elvis was about to inflate!

During 1976 Elvis never did slow down. It was one tour right after another. That worried me, and I began asking the Lord about Elvis' tempo.

"He's only running," the Lord wisely advised, "he's only running. And the faster he runs the sooner he'll run out of places to go and he'll run into Me."

I spoke with the Blackwood Brothers Quartet again in September. I told them what I knew and they assured me they were still praying.

As I talked to one member of the group who had known Elvis for years, I asked, "What do you think it would take to move Elvis . . . make him think about his own life and follow his calling?"

"An earthquake," he said and then added very solemnly, "actually it'd probably take his own death. Yes, that's probably what it would take . . . his own death."

I remembered the message I'd left with Hal and added, "That's just what I'm afraid of."

I sensed that things were building to a peak again because of the various Scriptures and incidences that had been increasing.

Again, I asked the Lord for a Scripture to help me understand where He was leading. I picked up my *Layman's Parallel Bible* and opened to a page that held only two Scriptures. They read nearly the same in all four translations. The King James version 2 Timothy 4:21-22 stated, "Do thy diligence to come before winter . . . The Lord Jesus Christ be with thy spirit. Grace be unto you. . . ."

The only message there coincided with the dream the Lord had given me with the suitcase. It looked as if I might be going somewhere before winter, and it was already the end of September.

A two-week period of silence followed, while my curiosity rose to an unbearable level. Then, as God began to deal with me, my spiritual eyes were opened to view two angels having a casual conversation.

It seemed I was being allowed to eavesdrop on their communication. As I listened, one stated, "Well, we know *one* thing for sure. If it's not done, either *God* can't do it . . . or *she* won't."

"Yes, that's right," the other one seconded. "You're absolutely correct."

As I analyzed the conversation I knew that God could do anything, so it seemed apparent that the "she" in question was me and the responsibility was mine too. And since it was probably my willingness that was in question I figured that I would be hearing *what* before much longer!

A few days later, while I sat in the kitchen studying the Bible, the Lord interrupted by asking, "Will you go anyplace I send you?"

In trying to be totally honest with Him I thought before answering. Eventually, I decided that if He wanted me someplace . . . wherever it was . . . then I'd probably be safer there than in a place of my choosing, out of His will.

"Would you give me $500 of your savings if and when I ask for it?" was His second question.

"Sure," I answered casually, realizing that if He posed two questions this far out then He must be testing me for some reason.

On October 31, 1976, an advertisement appeared in the travel section of the Kansas City paper concerning trips to Las Vegas, including tickets to the Elvis Presley show at the Las Vegas Hilton.

Jerry read the details while I paced the floor yelling, "What is the matter with him? Doesn't he know what he's doing? Doesn't he realize that he's playing with his own life?"

Inwardly, I already *knew* I was going to Las Vegas, although I denied it to the end. It wouldn't even be logical for me to go! But the guidance had all fallen into place and I had told Hal that if they were in Vegas again it was because the Lord wanted something accomplished.

I didn't say anything to Jerry concerning my inner thoughts, but he voiced his individual opinion by saying, "You're not going out there, so don't get any ideas."

"I will only if I have to . . . and that's the *only* way I'll go," I quickly responded as I prepared to go to Denise's house for a prearranged visit with her and two other friends.

7

EAGLES ARE FOR SOARING

"The moral of the story is, don't ever make a bargain with God and then try to back out of it!" I exclaimed as I walked briskly through Denise's front door.

With a laugh, she followed me into another room where the other ladies were sitting.

During our visit that day, the subject slowly swung to Elvis, as I related my concern for his well-being and the Las Vegas concerts I had just learned about that morning.

Later, when Jerry phoned to ask when I'd be home, I replied, "In a few minutes," and hung up the receiver.

Turning to leave, Betty interrupted me by saying, "You are to go."

"Yes, I have to go home," I replied in a casual tone.

"Sit back down," the Lord interrupted. "She's trying to tell you something."

Bracing myself, I cautiously asked, "What did you say to me, Betty?"

"You are to go," she smilingly reaffirmed.

"*To Las Vegas?*" I asked hysterically. Then after I had regained control of myself I asked, "Why are you so sure?"

"While you were talking to me I kept wondering how I was involved. Where did I fit in? It seemed you weren't just accidentally telling me this. Then I asked the Lord what I should do or say to help. So while you were on the phone He told me to tell you that you were to go. This is the right time," she methodically commented with a peaceful and content expression.

"Okay, but first the Lord will have to confirm every step of the way," I explained.

54

As the first confirmation began I was shown something the Lord told me symbolized Elvis' life. I observed a small sail-tattered ship tossing to and fro on a very foggy, stormy sea. The blinding blanket of fog was slowly receding into the calmer waters of a bay. Then the fog continued steadily lifting until the clouds began rolling back. Looking upward, I saw an opening in the heavy mist and Jesus pictured against the blue skies, reaching His arms down to guide the small storm-tossed vessel into the safety of the harbor.

As is the Lord's way, there was already enough preliminary evidence to suggest a trip to Vegas.

I had had an earlier dream in which I'd found the Las Vegas Hilton, and the one by a registration desk with suitcase in hand. Plus Betty's direct statement.

But the Lord hadn't spoken personally to me. That was my next request.

Deciding that I would give Him all the time He needed to respond the next day while I prayed. He quoted Isaiah 40:31, which states, "But they that wait upon the Lord shall renew their strength; they shall mount up with wings as eagles; they shall run, and not be weary; and they shall walk, and not faint."

Then momentarily He added, "What do you think 'mount up with wings as eagles' *could* mean in today's vernacular?"

I remained on my knees alternating between thoughts of adventure and moments of cowardice in anticipation of the response He wanted from me. After several minutes I suggested, "A jet?"

"Yes, a jet," He replied in a satisfied voice.

The adventurous feeling remained as I ran recklessly through the house to call Denise and tell her the Lord had just confirmed the trip.

In passing, I mentioned to the Lord that it would certainly be uplifting if another prophecy would be given to me before I had to go to Vegas.

Without any delay He unexpectedly remarked, "How about, 'Lift up your eyes, and look on the fields; for they are white already to harvest'?"

My mind immediately reflected on the many times I had earnestly prayed to reach Elvis only when he was ready.

As the days passed I had an increasing awareness that someone from out of town, who knew nothing about my plans, would phone and confirm my trip, too.

At two in the morning Alma phoned me from California to deliver a Scripture that the Lord had given her that afternoon during prayer. "Read 2 Timothy 4:6 in the King James Version and see if it might confirm something," she said.

After we had finished talking I read the Scripture. "For I am now ready to be offered, and the time of my departure is at hand." It definitely confirmed.

I had decided to try Sun World Travel first. I phoned to check on ticket availability and found I had plenty of time to wait. I planned a delay of several days in order to see if the best I could do was acceptable to the Lord.

He had been repeatedly saying, "Four days and three nights." But the longest trip I could find was three days and three nights.

I had also been told to "Go first class," but as far as my present knowledge went, that was impossible too.

The Lord chose to alter my tentative decision through still another dream.

That night I saw myself, Jerry, Denise, and her husband, Jerry, walking into a travel agency to pick up tickets. As we left, alarm buzzers began sounding warnings, alerting several policemen who chased us through a downtown area.

Finally, finding safety, I suggested that I take back the tickets and exchange them for one for me alone that fit my particular needs.

Returning to the agency, I explained the mix-up to an older man seated at a desk. He understood my problem and talked with me to his wife for a possible solution. Within minutes I had the correct ticket.

Now I knew I wasn't supposed to secure those travel arrangements and my idea of taking Denise or anyone else along was eliminated.

I had contacted the Savings Association for the $500 the Lord had been "testing" me about earlier! That check bounced all over Missouri before I finally received it two days before departure.

From the minute I knew Elvis was to be in Vegas, I knew I *had* to be there on the fifth of December, although he'd be there from the second to the twelfth.

I waited until I felt led to phone a different agency and checked on their flights for the fifth. They didn't have the proper number of days the Lord had been suggesting either, but then, neither did anyone else!

So I made tentative arrangements and was told the ticket would be ready for me the following evening, which was the second of December.

When Jerry and I arrived to pick up the papers I was greeted with the news that I couldn't get a flight, much less get a ticket to Elvis' show. After a proper apology for my inconvenience the clerk added, "However, there is a possible cancellation on the twelfth."

"The twelfth!" I complained in a hysterical voice. As I listened to her unbelievable statement I could have told her there wouldn't be a cancellation to Elvis' show unless someone died! I know the fans too well. Seeing the show wasn't the necessary ingredient now anyway, just getting there was the essential thing. Well, I concluded, the Lord will just have to do better than this.

After we had driven home I began trying to decide which airline to phone at Kansas City International Airport. I didn't even know *what* to ask! I'd never purchased an airline ticket in my life, much less tried to talk intelligently to the ticket agent.

My indecision only grew so I asked the Lord which airline to choose. "Fly the friendly skies . . ." He responded. I quickly added "United" and phoned them!

I found that the available seats on flight no. 555 leaving December fifth at 9:45 A.M. had a round trip price of $328. They urged me to reserve one of the few remaining seats.

I had to decline their offer, too. The Lord had allotted $500, so why was the ticket so expensive? There had to be another plan someplace.

On December third, I phoned Denise and related the story. "There is absolutely no logical, available way for me to fly to Las Vegas and be there by the fifth. Much less be there four days, three nights, go to the show, or first class! Basically, we need a miracle. It's too late to drive, and besides the Lord said fly! God is the only one able to straighten this thing out in the next forty-eight hours. So give me fifteen minutes to read a chapter in a book and call the travel agency again. Then start praying with me and let's claim Matthew 18:19."

As always, Denise said she would be in prayer.

I hurried downstairs and located Harold Hill's book, *How to be a Winner*, and read chapter sixteen that I had just remembered was titled, "How to be a Winner over the High Cost of Flying and Hotel No-Vacancy Signs." If God had done it for one King's kid, then He could do it for another! Harold Hill's circumstances had varied somewhat from mine. But the same working principle was used. Faith in God.

I dialed the agency that had failed to make necessary connections two days earlier requesting, "I *have* to be in Vegas on the fifth. Can you arrange it? I need a flight, plus four days and three nights in a private room, and other incidentals that you know more about than I do!"

"I'll try, but I can't promise anything on such short notice," she cautioned.

After thirty minutes of prayer, the Lord allowed me to see Satan in my mind's eye. He appeared as a red figure bending over in front of me. In my hands was a large club that I raised and broke across his back in a crushing blow. As a result he took off running and screaming with his hands flailing the air.

With an ecstatic reaction I phoned Denise exclaiming, "We've broken through! I can't wait for them to call me, I have to phone them!"

I dialed the number and quickly asked to speak to Rosemary. She confirmed what I already knew by saying, "I just secured passage for you on flight no. 555 leaving at 9:45 A.M. on December fifth and returning four days later. But the price will be higher for one person travelling alone rather than in the groups."

Remembering the price was $151 in groups, I held my breath asking, "Okay, what is it?"

As I waited for her to check I knew I would have to pay whatever she asked and go in order to even get out there.

"The cost is $164," she replied regretfully.

My mouth flew open! Same flight, same day, same departure . . . but half-price? That had to be the Lord.

"May I pick up the ticket in the morning?" I suggested.

"It'll have to be afternoon, because since this is such short notice we'll have to go get the ticket for you at the airport. Do you have a hotel preference?" she said.

"I don't really have a preference, just find a hotel and a single room," I replied.

On Saturday morning before we left to go to Carpentours Travel Agency and pick up the ticket, Jerry began wavering somewhat in allowing me to go. I sensed his feelings as he avoided the subject, and quickly asked the Lord to intervene.

Within a few minutes after Jerry had walked into another room to prepare to leave, he returned with a blank expression on his face. "Do you know what the Lord just said to me?" he asked in a slow questioning tone.

"No," I replied and waited for him to tell me.

"He told me to let you alone, and let you go." Then he added in a convincing voice, "Because He said this was a great work . . . His work."

After the Lord had spoken to Jerry there was no more doubt in his mind concerning my safety, or whether or not the Lord was sending me.

I debated telling Susan, my neighbor, and I had decided to leave the decision in the Lord's hands with the understanding that if it was unavoidable I would tell her.

At ten o'clock the night of December fourth the doorbell rang. It was Susan holding a jar for Jerry to open for her!

When she walked by me and looked curiously at the stack of papers on the table in front of me I knew this was the "unavoidable" I had requested.

"What are you doing?" she asked suspiciously.

"Flying to Las Vegas," I replied, waiting to see if she could figure out the rest.

"To see Elvis?" she inquired.

"Yes, and I'll need your prayers," I explained, adding that I'd asked the Lord to lead her to me if I was to tell her.

"You've got 'em," she responded. "I'll be praying for you."

That night the word sleep completely left my vocabulary. I lay in bed praying until four A.M. and finally decided I should get ready to leave for the airport.

I phoned Kate, a friend of mine who had helped pray for Elvis and Hal off and on over the past three years.

"Don't say a word!" I exclaimed as Kate answered the phone, "Just listen! I'm leaving for Las Vegas in three hours to see Elvis. I'm going alone. The Lord has made that clear. I can't even take Denise with me. This is the time and I have to go. I've received every conceivable confirmation over the past several weeks. But I need your prayers."

"I'm not saying anything," she nervously answered, "but I sure am thinking fast! And I definitely intend to pray!"

Later she shared that she immediately began asking the Lord to break my leg if necessary in order to keep me off that jet.

The next day when she had calmed down the Lord asked her to read Isaiah 61:1 which reads, "The Spirit of the Lord is upon me; because the Lord hath anointed me to preach good tidings unto the meek; he hath sent me to bind up the brokenhearted, to proclaim liberty to the captives, and the opening of the prison to them that are bound." It was then that she realized that it had been time for me to go to Elvis.

As we began driving to the airport I mentally turned around every quarter mile! Here I am, I thought to myself, going to Las Vegas . . . alone. I haven't even been on an airplane, or in an airport. I'm afraid of heights, and I'm capable of getting completely lost within the confines of an elevator!

The only thing positive in Las Vegas was Hal knew I was coming. We had exchanged calls during the last three days and I alerted him to the fact that the Lord was sending me to Vegas. And if he could get some guy named Elvis Presley out of town I might be able to get a flight and a hotel room!

8

LAS VEGAS

Deafening silence had reigned supreme during the previous twenty-four hours. Then, as I walked through the corridor to board the plane, the Lord's voice pierced the stillness as He made His presence known.

His reassuring tone brought the realization that He knew my apprehension as these words came to my mind. "Go to it, kid! There's an angel on each side of you. Go get 'em!"

More welcome orders were never received! My fears faded and instead of uncertainty I found myself restraining the urge to run the rest of the way to the jet.

As I walked down the aisle of the plane I realized I didn't know how to locate my seat. I dreaded looking totally ignorant of the entire procedure, so I asked the Lord for assistance.

Almost before I could finish asking, a man stood up from behind a row of seats, secured my attention, and asked, "Do you have seat 8F?"

The number sounded familiar, so I reached for my ticket to check. "Yes, it's 8F," I said in amazement while he pointed to the correct seat.

"These seating systems are difficult to read when you're not used to them," he added.

As the jet lifted off and circled the airport I began grinning from ear-to-ear and I didn't stop until after we landed in Vegas!

My faith became as elevated as the plane was as I read the words of faith in the Bible and a book on faith by Chris Panos titled *Faith under Fire*.

McCarren Airport in Las Vegas was new territory for me and I didn't necessarily want to start out by getting lost! Therefore, for the second time I requested help from the Lord in the form of a person to help me after we landed.

He readily assured me that He would move someone to the aisle seat behind me.

Midway into the flight when an older man sat down in the previously assigned chair, the Lord said, "That's him. That's the man I spoke about."

"Okay, have him say something to me for verification," I replied.

Momentarily, the man turned to me requesting, "Do you have anything interesting to read?"

I paused a second to thank the Lord for a perfect question before answering, "Yes, I think so. I have my Bible, there's any kind of story you want to read in it. And a book on faith."

"You've got a what?" he retorted in disbelief that anyone heading for Vegas could be a Christian.

"A Bible and a book on faith," I repeated.

He slowly turned his head and with a slight smile ignored my second answer.

"Lord," I complained, "allow him to ask for my ink pen since he's not a Christian. Then I'll know You picked him even if he isn't Yours."

Within seconds the man tapped my shoulder asking, "I hate to keep bothering you again. But I seem to have lost my ink pen. Do you have one I could borrow for a moment?"

"I sure do," I replied with a smile that I know he didn't understand.

He quickly used the pen to write a short note and then placed the note and the pen in his pocket.

"Lord, he put my pen in his pocket," I reasoned. "It's not the pen itself that's important, but it's the one Alma gave to me before she left for California and I want it back. Could You talk to him again?"

For the third time the man responded by reaching in his coat and handing me the pen. "I'm sorry I forgot, forgive me," he pleaded.

"That's all right," I said, realizing that someone would be available when we landed.

After our brief encounter, the man moved to a seat out of my view and never spoke with me again during the flight.

I looked casually across the empty seats dividing the aisle to exchange greetings with a couple that for some reason seemed familiar.

As our plane touched down, I glanced out my window and discovered Elvis' Convair 880 jet setting by the side, complete with a lightning bolt and Takin' Care of Business motto on its tail.

Needless to say, I radiated pure satisfaction that the Lord and I had at last arrived, totally intact, despite all the interference during the last few days!

While the plane taxied to the terminal I found myself recalling the vision of the Hilton and the one only eight months earlier where I'd been beside a hotel registration desk holding a suitcase. Even the color of those cases and the color of my new ones coincided. Without any planning, even that small detail was carefully fulfilled.

As we filed into a line to leave the plane a voice behind me interrupted my thoughts by asking, "What brought you out here?"

I turned to find the man from the aisle seat standing behind me. "The Lord sent me," I explained.

"Well, if you came out here for Him," he said with a grin and a shake of the head, "you certainly came to the right place!"

"You think I've found a fish bowl, do you?" I inquired.

"I definitely do! I definitely do!" he stressed.

"Are you going to see any of the shows while you're out here?" he questioned.

"No, I don't believe I will. Well . . . possibly Elvis'. I'm not sure," I answered.

"Oh, you like Elvis do you?" he asked while smiling sheepishly.

"Yes, I guess you could say I like Elvis," I confessed. "As a matter-of-fact, Elvis is the one the Lord sent me out here to talk to!" Then it was my turn to smile sheepishly while he tried to comprehend my statement.

"By the way, the Lord answered a prayer on the plane by sending you to sit down behind me," I explained as we walked through the airport.

"Me?" he exclaimed.

"Yes, you see I've never been here before and I needed help through the terminal and as you can see, you're helping me."

He looked amazed. People just can't seem to comprehend God's subtle way of manipulating circumstances for His kids.

"You know the Lord has everything and everyone within His grasp," I continued, "and He's just waiting for each one of us to give Him total control of our lives."

Abruptly changing the subject he asked, "Are you going to at least try the slot machines while you're here?"

"No," I replied. "When you have a 'sure thing' going it would be ridiculous to gamble or take any unnecessary risks."

He turned quickly and looked at me as if I might know something that he didn't know.

Answering his unasked question, I continued, "I mean, what the Lord says about giving."

With that he began shaking his head in an "Oh, no, not again" fashion.

But I ignored his uneasiness and continued. "You know the Bible says in Malachi that when you give to God that He'll return such a blessing that you can't even receive it all!"

He turned his head and mumbled something about his sister who went to the bank, and someone else's prayers. I read between the lines and came to the conclusion that the Lord had us on that flight for more than one reason!

After he assisted me in finding my luggage and locating the correct door to walk out, we parted.

"Are you Mary Ann Thornton?" a man inquired as I walked out the double doors.

"Yes," I answered, as he led me to a limousine.

During the drive to the hotel I asked the driver where it was located in distance from the Hilton.

"The Landmark is directly across from it," he answered.

"Great!" I replied, happily recalling that I'd given the agency no preferences.

From there my mind wandered to a comparison between the trip I could have gotten and the one the Lord arranged. The other trip was a group flight, a double room in a lower quality hotel for three days and two nights. After some juggling the Lord arranged a trip to His specifications consisting of a single room and an airline ticket for four days and three nights at a better hotel.

Who could complain for six dollars difference?

I turned to walk into the Landmark after I'd mischievously saluted toward the Hilton . . . just in case Elvis was watching!

Following precise instructions, I found a phone and called home. After calling Jerry I dialed Denise's number.

"Is the registration desk the one the Lord showed you before?" she yelled over the phone.

"I don't know, I forgot to look. Just a second and I'll see,"

I replied while straining across the casino. "Yep! That's it," I confidently replied.

"Oh, praise God!" came her usual raptured reply. "I've been dying to ask you that!"

After depositing my luggage in room 1401 I walked to the Hilton to locate Hal, only to find "Do Not Disturb" signs and messages everyplace I looked.

I went back to my room and asked the Lord to get ahold of Hal one more time. I also reminded Him that I didn't believe He'd sent me fourteen hundred miles so I could experience sitting in a hotel room in the middle of the desert for four days. I prayed and waited.

Later that afternoon the Lord told me when to go back to the Hilton. This time He told me to take the elevator to the twenty-first floor and knock on Hal's door, sign or no sign.

"What are you doing out here?" Hal asked as if he hadn't known I was coming.

"I told you the Lord was sending me. Don't you remember? I talked to you three times before I came!" I reminded him.

"I'm going home anyway," I demanded. "I don't like it out here. I feel totally disoriented."

"Whoa! You can't go now. Get in here!" he said while dragging me into the room.

"All right, let me give you an update," I said and sat down to give him a detailed account of everything the Lord had maneuvered during the past months in order to convince me to come to Vegas.

When I finished, the Lord's presence had filled the room. With misty eyes and a sincere curiosity he asked, "The Lord really did *all* that? Just so you could come out here and talk to us?"

"Yes," I assured him, "He did that and much more."

That led to a lengthy conversation concerning the Lord's ways culminating in an invitation to church.

I'd contacted a church in Las Vegas for their prayer support on that Sunday night and added that I'd attend if I wasn't at the Hilton.

"Come, go to church with me tonight," I suggested.

"I can't. I have a show to do," he quickly replied and dropped into deep thought before suggesting, "Come down to the dressing room with us tonight. We leave here about eight-thirty. Stay and have supper with us and it'll be all right for you to go to the downstairs area."

I mentally asked the Lord for what I knew would be a denial. "Go ahead," was His unexpected answer.

"Sure, I'll go with you," I solemnly replied to Hal, wondering what possible good that could do.

The desert air and Hal's health had been clashing to the degree that he had received medical attention and was needing it again.

"Do you want me to pray for you instead?" I inquired.

"Yes, will you?"

The Lord's presence prevailed in such a way as I ministered to Hal that there was no doubt that God's healing power was in operation. As I finished, tears were trickling down Hal's cheeks and his ability to talk was limited to praises to God.

Moments later Hal asked for a drink of something, as the doctor had prescribed.

"The Lord healed you! Drink whatever you want in whatever way you want," I firmly stated.

Hal suddenly turned and looked at me as if I had read his mind. Although he failed to disclose his condition, no doctors were contacted.

When our conversation lapsed into small talk, Hal began discussing his annoyance about a sum of money that Richard, a friend, had "borrowed without permission" during the previous night while he had been upstairs walking the floor with a disturbed Elvis.

"Richard needs prayer instead of any humiliation," I suggested and the Lord nudged me to add, "I'll tell you what. You let me pray for Richard and the Lord will help him, but besides that as a sign to you, he'll be out of town in twenty-four hours."

"Richard? He's too obnoxious to leave. He turns up wherever we are," Hal remarked with an angry frown.

I was concerned by the way Hal had said Elvis was talking. One incident that relates the overall attitude was after Elvis had paced the floor, he stopped beside the full-length windows of his thirtieth floor suite gazing upon the brilliant night lights of Las Vegas. Turning to Hal, Elvis shook his head slowly and asked remorsefully, "What do you do? What do you do? When you know you could buy everything out there that your eyes fell on . . . and you're still unhappy? Where do you go next?"

Around eight-thirty that night we walked to the dressing rooms through back halls and down service elevators until we reached our destination.

As I turned to walk down the stairs into the basement, I recognized the hall and the doors from a vision I'd received shortly before Elvis' 1976 concert in Kansas City. Everything I was seeing was familiar and the next activity in that vision was finding Elvis.

After preliminary introductions had been made and old acquaintances greeted, I sat down and began talking with a girl that I discovered had been sent to Las Vegas by her "church" to convert Elvis. It *is* a religion that encouraged her, but religion isn't necessarily Christianity.

I should have expected something like this! It was almost a pattern. The Lord's requirements were for me to sit, be neutral, compassionate, and counsel her. Which, of course, I did.

While I talked with her she began nervously watching the doorway. Out of curiosity, I turned to find Lisa, Elvis' daughter, standing there watching me.

Eventually we exchanged messages. Part vocal, part silent.

Throughout the evening the Holy Spirit repeatedly said, "This is it," to me.

My only question was, "This is what?"

While I visited with the different members of the group, Hal sat at the opposite end of the room talking with a musician with a bandaged eye.

The next thing I knew, Hal and the guitar player were walking toward me. Hal asked him to sit down in front of me and then asked, "Will you pray for him?"

"Sure," I replied and Hal reached for a chair for him to sit in.

Again God's presence was overwhelming like it had been that afternoon as Hal and I talked. As I continued praying his facial expression told me that God had touched him spiritually as well as physically.

The next time he walked through the dressing room his patch had been discarded.

Finally Richard made an appearance. He walked in, Hal yelled, and I remembered the twenty-four hours and hoped God intended to answer quickly.

Before long the scene repeated itself and I was asked to pray for Richard.

"It would do you good to spend thirty minutes talking to her about God," Hal instructed.

Then turning to me, Hal requested, "Will you pray for him now?"

Again I answered affirmatively. God doesn't call Christians to make decisions about who and where they will pray for people. He calls them to minister anyplace they are needed, and I was about to find that out!

Instead of reaching for the chair again, Hal motioned for me to follow them. After walking a few steps, we turned a corner . . . Lord? not the restroom! That was just about enough!! I rolled my eyes and slipped into a mild state of shock while I reluctantly continued.

"She's going to pray for you now, Richard," Hal stated reverently. "And it will do you a world of good, you'll see. She came out here to help . . . even if it's just me and you. She doesn't even care whether she sees Elvis or not. She came to help whomever she could."

In this predicament I didn't know what to do, but I did know the Lord could minister anyplace.

"Hal, I want you to pray too," I asked and began praying for Richard's salvation.

After I had prayed in the rather crowded quarters, Hal very emotionally added a beautiful finish to the prayer requesting victory in Richard's life.

That evening Richard told me he had finished two Bible Colleges, but hadn't followed up in the ministry. Then he began revealing a long list of celebrities who had once been engaged in the Lord's work.

After the show, Richard borrowed $200 from a member of the group and left Vegas within twenty-four hours fulfilling the earlier statement.

Another member of Elvis' group from Memphis walked in. (For the sake of privacy he'll be referred to as Len throughout the story.) As he strolled past me he suddenly turned and seemingly recognized me.

"Hi, Len," I called.

"Well, hello again. How are you?" he responded on the way over to talk to Hal.

Again I watched while he talked to Len and began pointing toward me.

And within minutes I was asked to pray for Len. I excused myself and went back to the "office" with them.

The way the Lord had ministered to Richard, He didn't mind, so who was I to start making the decisions now? If there had been anyplace else offering any privacy, I would have been the first to suggest it. But there simply wasn't.

Over the years I'd heard specific things about Len, including that he had once been with one of the nation's leading evangelists. I wanted to pray as effectively as I could so I waited until I could remember some of his past.

During the prayer a word of knowledge surfaced that went past my own knowledge. It stated, "Lord, I feel there's something blocking the pure flow of Your Spirit. Begin a work in Len's life and remove the obstruction."

When I concluded, tears began rolling down Len's cheeks as he reached and hugged me, then with a strained voice he added, "It's been a long time since I've felt anything like that."

"Praise God, Len," I urged as we began walking slowly toward the door.

Len paused and turned to me with a sincere expression, requesting, "Wait a minute, you just gave me something. Now I want to give you something in return."

"All right, but what is it first?" I questioned.

Slowly and deliberately, Len placed one hand on either side of my face and looked deeply into my eyes with intense concentration. "Do you feel that heat?" he asked with a satisfied smile.

"Yes, I feel it. Why?" I replied after I'd felt a strange warmth. Glancing toward Hal I saw that he was smiling approvingly instead of realizing that this was wrong.

"Well, you see, I'm a psychic healer," he confidently assured me.

My prayer line was cleared for immediate service as I shot a quick S.O.S. toward the throne. "Okay, Lord. You and I are in this mess together because You sent me here. Now, how do You expect me to get out of this? Gracefully or otherwise?" (At least now I knew what the blockage was that had been mentioned during the prayer.)

The Lord calmly replied, "Just stand there and plead the blood of Jesus out loud while you silently pray back on him what he's trying to give to you."

Len was determined to help me and I was determined that he wasn't! Yet not a word was exchanged openly. It wasn't the man being rebuked, so his feelings weren't hurt.

Later in the evening I told Len that his psychic powers were wrong. We agreed that we could disagree because we were friends. One thing we need to remember is that to help someone you must be able to communicate with them. Jesus never abused anyone's feelings, instead He was welcomed by publicans and respected for His overwhelming love and honesty.

After I had reentered the main section of the room, one of Elvis' business associates began discussing underlying relationships with me, including some things about Hal.

"I'm glad you came out here," he shared, "you know Hal has been under such conviction for the past three years that he's been nearly impossible to live with at times! All he needs is a little extra shove and he'll be in . . . and we'll loose him. But he needs God."

"Hal? He has?" I inquired with a startled expression. "Great! Because it just so happens that I've been praying for him for the past three years."

He turned pale immediately and avoided the subject for the remainder of the evening. I guess he had been happy I came, but he wasn't going to tell me too much.

Len was in and out of the dressing room all evening long, looking much like the proverbial yo-yo.

After the hallway had been cleared for thirty minutes for security reasons, Elvis came down to prepare for the show.

Len left the dressing room for the last time after he casually stopped in front of me just long enough to say, "Well, it's time to wind him up and turn him loose." Then with a wink he left.

Since I knew that Len helped Elvis prepare for shows, he was evidently closer than I thought.

9

AN EFFECTUAL DOOR

During Elvis' performance that night he sang, "How Great Thou Art." That was one song he could do justice when he wanted to!

Yet, I've never heard him sing it as movingly as he did that night at the Hilton as the words "How Great" in his own phrasing of "How great I think You are, Oh, Lord," were repeated five times. Each one crescendoing until his voice cracked in the strain to deliver the descent of the note.

After the concert everyone regathered in the dressing room. We began discussing religion and God.

Everything was peaceful until several of those in the room became upset over the accuracy of the answers the Holy Spirit was giving me.

Consequently the subject was turned to accusing questions as I was asked if I'd ever taken my spirit from my body by my "own power," didn't I know that the Apostle Paul was a homosexual, and didn't I feel that Jesus and Mary had a love affair. You name it and I was asked it! My firm denials of their suggestions brought mounting friction.

Moses was mentioned in a scriptural reference in one of the answers I gave. Then one of the men boldly told me that he'd been an acquaintance of Moses in another life.

Looking at him and addressing the source of his deception I affirmed, "Yes, I'm sure you did too."

The Holy Spirit reminded me of the Scripture the Lord had been repeatedly giving to me during the few days before I left. A comparison had been made between the resistance I'd encounter to the way Jannes and Jambres withstood Moses in

Pharaoh's court (2 Timothy 3:8 and Exodus 7:11-12) by implementing the power of the "gods of Egypt."

I knew this mortal man couldn't have known Moses because there is "no other life" (Hebrews 9:27), but the same force that was present in Moses' day was here, too.

The Gospel became so eroded and their ears became so closed to the truth that I couldn't listen any longer.

"I'll go home then if that's the way you *really* feel about it!" I stated as I stood up to leave.

"Oh, no you don't! You can't go home. Not now!" Len and Hal chimed as they grasped my arms and sat me down again.

After another accusation of having patented answers before the questions were fully asked, I explained, "But you see, the Holy Spirit knows the answer *before* you ask anything. It's not me, it's His guidance and I can't block the flow of answers."

Within minutes I excused myself and walked into the restroom alone. I had to talk to God.

"Lord," I began, "You and I both know that You didn't send me out here to risk my life, not to even mention my reputation for *this!* I could have stayed in Kansas City and eventually seen Elvis in concert again. So if You have to open every door in this hotel to get me in to Elvis, or go directly through him, or move every person sitting out there, then *please* do it! If that's the only way it can be accomplished, I know You have the power to do it, so please do it."

As I walked back into the room, it had quieted immensely from the previous conversation. I sat down and began encouraging myself with the vision I'd received during June of 1975 when I'd seen the gates in front of the Hilton that weren't there naturally. And how I had taken authority over the forces by using Jesus' name. Those gates had swung open. I wondered if that was what had just happened!

A surge of God's presence caused me to begin silently praying. Hal was talking and became frustrated because my eyes were closed and he no longer had my undivided attention. What he didn't know is that I was doing everything within my power to remain that passive!

After Hal had finished giving a long list of reasons why God allowed his sins, he asked two others if they'd allow me to pray with them. Then turning to me, he said, "Don't worry, I'll make it to Heaven."

I didn't answer his foolishness. Instead I just looked at him.

72

His facial expression began to show the guilt and shame that comes with denying Christ.

The two girls that Hal had asked me to pray for were both eager. But instead of making an exhibition of their prayers I suggested we hold hands and form a circle to pray.

I'd prayed so many lengthy prayers that I felt I'd exhausted the supply of words. Again I asked the Lord for words of wisdom for these people who needed Him so desperately.

"Go on, pray," Hal urged, shaking my arm.

"Just a minute," I quietly reasoned and put my mind on the Lord again.

"Go on and pray," Hal impatiently demanded.

As I had waited the Lord's power rested on me with an increasing intensity, bringing about a physical reaction that caused me to begin trembling in expectation.

With a peace that passed understanding, I opened my mouth to pray, but instead found myself calling out in a bold voice, "God. MOVE!"

While the words were yet in mid-air it seemed the flood gates of Heaven had been opened.

The dozen or so people in the room began feeling the same things I'd felt only moments earlier. Then almost immediately after I yielded, the Holy Spirit began using me to give a message in tongues (1 Corinthians 12:10).

Throughout the message Hal kept squeezing my right hand, saying with intense emphasis, "That's real, that's real."

And a musician standing to my left was swinging my other hand in tempo to repeated phrases of, "Bless her, Lord, bless her."

While Len began simultaneously exclaiming, "That's Hebrew! That's Hebrew!"

One girl ran out of the dressing room sobbing and openly calling upon God, while the others remained behind and wept.

As the message came to a close I waited for the interpretation.

After the acceptable break in speaking, the Lord gave the interpretation that fitted the evening together perfectly.

His word to them was, *If you will walk toward My outstretched arms, I have more for each of you than any one of you can comprehend or believe.*

I will lead you, I will guide you, I will protect you with the saving strength of My right arm.

There will be rivers of life opened up in the desert and I will

73

turn your sorrow into joy, your guilt into repentance, and take upon Myself your cares.

I love each of you and I long to hear praises to Me leave your lips and sail Heavenward.

I was elated that God would reveal Himself like this to them. Suddenly, a torrent of praises began to roll from me thanking Him for His compassion.

"Be still!" Hal cautioned while placing his hand over my mouth and glancing nervously to the doorway. "Elvis will think we're killing you over here!"

"Don't bother me," I said, still laughing joyously, "right at this moment what Elvis thinks is the furtherest thing from my mind." But I did wonder why Hal had said "over here"!

With outstretched hands Len assisted me to my chair. The effect of the Lord's power was still obvious as I sighed and added, "Now *that's* high!" And as they all looked at one another suspiciously I added, "And you know what, there's no bad after effects in the morning. Nothing but more peace!"

Each person appeared amazed at how God had revealed His power as they stood in small groups discussing it or asking me questions.

Finally I asked Hal if I should explain that two gifts of the Spirit had been in operation.

"No, never explain God," he exclaimed, "everyone in this room knows what that was."

After everyone except Hal, his girl friend, and I had left the room, Hal walked out.

As she and I sat waiting for him to return the Holy Spirit used the time to continue repeating, "This is it."

I had thought all the activity had ceased for one evening, but He was still alerting me, so to the discomfort of the girl with me, I began to freshen up for whatever was ahead.

"Where did Hal go?" I asked.

"Oh, somewhere," she stiffly replied.

"When will he be back?" I asked, "I'm tired. I've been up over twenty-four hours and I don't know how much longer I can stay awake."

Within a few minutes a guard knocked on the dressing room door.

She opened it and we were asked to step into the hall.

Three security guards watched us until the door across the hall opened and she was asked to come in.

"What about her?" she cautiously inquired, glancing toward me.

"She'll have to stay out there," came the faint reply.

The door closed behind her as the guards informed me, "You can't stand out in the hall."

"Okay, I don't want you to get into any trouble," I stated as they turned the key in the lock.

Several minutes passed before I was asked to come into the hall again.

"Come on in now, it's okay," came the request from Hal's girl friend.

I walked through the door behind her, bracing myself while I wondered if "This is it."

We walked through the door on our left that led to a large room with a game table in the center. Just like in the vision I'd had before Elvis' 1976 Kansas City concert.

Hal found a chair for me and we were seated at the table. I tried to talk to him, but he wouldn't respond. Instead, he seemed to be angry!

So I turned my attention to a painting hanging to my right. It was a vivid red and white reproduction of a pure white cross with the name John forcibly scrawled in red on the vertical beam. The man who had complimented the canvas with his artistry seemed to want to convey that all the judgment in existence had poured down upon it. It was signed, but when I made a conversational point out of it, not one person would second what I already had seen.

Glancing around the room I recognized several of Elvis' entourage and tentatively decided that this was a quiet after-the-show party that I'd been allowed to attend because I'd been with Hal and his girl friend.

I began admiring a poinsettia placed on the table. I casually reached for the attached card. Turning it over I read, "To Elvis Presley, c/o Imperial Suite, Las Vegas Hilton."

While I let the card slowly slip from between my fingers, I knew I was at least getting closer to wherever Elvis was. As my mind wandered I resolved that the Lord had allowed me this far tonight, and who knows, before I leave I'll probably have a chance to speak briefly with Elvis.

Before my decision had time to become settled one of the guys called across the room, "Hey, is Elvis still talking to his Dad?"

"Yeah, I think he is. Anyway he was," came the casual reply.

As I digested that a door to my left opened. When I glanced up there stood Elvis' Dad, Vernon. My immediate prayer was for him to remember me from the 1974 concert in Kansas City.

As he walked over and sat down beside me our eyes met with an instant recognition.

"Hello," I quietly responded.

"Yeah, hi," he said in a fading voice.

I slowly turned my eyes back toward the painting I had been studying for the last few minutes, while I examined the obvious evidence that Elvis was standing inside the adjacent room.

10

APPOINTMENT WITH DESTINY

The focal point of everyone's attention changed as a velvet hush swept across the crowded room.

Slowly dropping my eyes, I turned to Hal's girl friend. With a pleased smile on her face she turned to look at me and with an enticing gleam in her eyes told me I should follow her gaze, she looked toward the doorway Vernon had come through.

Before I looked, I lowered my head to the floor and committed the remainder of the night to the Lord.

"Thank You for answering my prayers and for not giving up on me when I was impatient and thought I wanted to quit. Thank You, Lord, for allowing me to do something I've sensed I should do since I was seven years old," I whispered.

After a million other thoughts penetrated my mind, I slowly raised my head and looked at the doorway. Elvis was standing beside Hal looking toward the opposite end of the room. He had lost quite a bit of weight, but he was so pale and sickly in appearance.

"Where is she?" Elvis asked him. No answer was given as Elvis looked across the room toward the table where I was seated.

As his eyes passed over me in expectation, he suddenly lowered his head and our eyes met with instant acknowledgment. With a persisting determination he held his fixed gaze and pointed toward me. "You," he confidently requested, "come here."

"Me?" I questioned, pointing at myself.

"Yes . . . you," he satisfactorily affirmed while he waited.

The only obvious problem that I had now was walking gracefully across the room, because now everyone was watching me instead of Elvis.

As I walked to the door, he walked to yet another doorway, and motioned for me to continue following him.

Once inside his private dressing room, Elvis slumped into a chair and folded his hands between his knees looking as if he was emotionally and physically exhausted.

I leaned against the wall and waited to see if Hal and Len were going to follow us. They walked in and Hal stood beside Elvis and requested that I stand in front.

Hal patted him on the shoulder softly, and assuringly said, "Elvis, this is Mary Ann."

"I know," he replied with a sigh of relief.

"She came out here to help you," Hal explained compassionately, "and she *is* real, Elvis."

With an upward glance accompanied by a nod, Elvis illustrated his acceptance.

"She prayed for me this afternoon and the Lord helped me. Elvis, I want you to know that if she hadn't prayed, I wouldn't have been able to make the show tonight, and you know what that would have meant." Hal glanced at me as he vocally confessed that God had touched him. "She's going to pray for you now. That's the only reason why she came. And it will help you, you'll see. Now go ahead and pray," Hal urged as he turned to me.

"Wait a minute, please," I quietly reasoned, knowing that Elvis had to want help before God would intervene. If Elvis wanted prayer, then that opened the door for all of God's necessary actions. If he didn't I was wasting my time.

"Elvis," I cautiously began, realizing his answer held the keys to the evening's results. "Do *you* want me to pray for you? That's the important part. Not that Hal or I want to help you, but do you want God to help you?"

"Yes, I do, very much so," Elvis humbly replied while continuing to look toward the floor.

I anxiously asked the Lord how I could get him to look at me and talk without bluntly asking.

"Get down on his level," came the Lord's unanticipated reply.

Human logic at first repelled the thought, but the compassion in the Lord's voice as He added, "Get down on your knees and talk to him," assured me that this was what He wanted.

"Elvis?" I tensely inquired, holding out my hand.

Without words he looked at me perceptively and reached to grasp my hands in much the same way a small frightened child would do.

As tears welled-up in his eyes, I asked, "What's wrong, Elvis? What's wrong? I only want to help. Regardless of what it is, God wants to change it."

With a distant gaze, he shrugged his shoulders in a "what's the use" attitude adding, "Oh . . . nothin'."

"Yes, there is, too, and you know it as well as I do," I quickly replied.

He looked toward me with a self-evaluating expression while nodding in agreement.

"Are you all right? Are you happy?" I asked.

"Happy? Huh . . . what's that?" he replied in a bitter voice.

"Elvis, I don't want to impose on you, now or ever. Do you really want God's help or are you just being nice? I don't want your politeness. I want honesty," I implored. "Believe me, nothing you could say to me would offend me."

Bowing his head in consent he replied, "Yes, please pray for me."

As I stood to my feet looking steadfastly toward Heaven I praised God for His faithfulness and asked for His presence to fill the room before I uttered one word in prayer.

The Holy Spirit immediately began moving into the room until it was as if all the words in the world were worthless and inadequate. And still God's power continued rushing in until even the air vibrated with His presence.

As I reached out to lay hands on Elvis' head, he began to tremble in reaction to the third member of the Trinity. The words I prayed didn't seem to be mine, instead they too seemed to be flowing in from a higher source. In retrospect, they almost seem prophetic in content.

"*Lord, You're the Alpha and the Omega,*" I began as a river of exhortations issued forth, "*You're the beginning and the ending, the author and the finisher of our faith. The Lord of the universe, wonderful, counsellor, the mighty God, the everlasting Father, the prince of peace, the lily of the valley, the bright and morning star, the creator and the redeemer, the Lamb of God who takes away the sin of the world, the Rose of Sharon, the Lord of lords and the reigning King of kings.*

With You, Lord, there is no changing or variance of way. And for these we praise You.

Lord, I've done all I can do. You've been faithful to fulfill all of Your promises. All I can do now is to take Elvis and lay him at Your feet and ask You to complete the work. Finish it, Lord.

The rest is in Your hands.

You are love, Lord so love him to Yourself. Let him know how much You love him the way You have shown me over and over again. Minister to him Lord because he is reaching out to You. Your Word says that those who come to You, will in no wise be cast out Lord, and I'm claiming that promise tonight.

Without You we're nothing . . . a speck of dust, a split second on the hands of time, we realize this more and more each day.

Elvis has asked for Your help, Lord. So begin a work in his life this minute to make his crooked places straight and provide a way of escape as the Word says You will do. Glorify Yourself, Lord. Take his hand and lead him home.

Let Your presence and Your power flow through every fiber of his being and every crevice of his soul. Bless him with an everlasting blessing even as I pray, Lord. Reach down and touch him. Cause a deeper stirring in his soul than he's ever known before. Create in him a hunger for Your Word and lead him.

Lord, YOU always prepare a way of escape for us no matter how black the night may become or how difficult our circumstances may seem. Prepare him for his escape, Lord.

We know that we have fallen short of Your goals for us because Your Word tells us we've all sinned and come short of Your glory. But forgive us . . . restore us . . . and return us to the God of our childhood."

As I prayed the application changed to Elvis alone. As I prayed for his soul he altered from his previous course of soft praises to the Lord and with a strained voice, through weeping, he softly asserted, "Please, forgive me, Lord. I'm so sorry. So sorry . . . please, forgive me. Please, help me, just help me."

Continuing to petition God, I was careful to listen attentively to what Elvis was telling the Lord, and still allow him the privacy of his own requests. After all, what he was saying wasn't exactly for me anyway.

Hot tears had involuntarily rolled from my eyes in streams as I prayed. As I opened them to look at Elvis while he made his requests, I realized that the tears I'd shed had been landing on his head forming wet creases in his hair.

Unless you were present, it's impossible to express just how gracious the Lord's presence was.

Then suddenly I saw Jesus standing behind Elvis silently giving me authority to continue praying through an all-knowing expression.

As His hand rested on Elvis' head, He firmly commanded, "Bind Satan's interference in his life."

"Anything but that, Lord." I sighed, recalling Elvis' sporadic temper. I could almost see myself sailing out through the narrow folding doors after I'd been properly attacked with everything his karate lessons had taught him!

However, an order is an order, so I addressed Satan. Bound his activities in Elvis' life, quoted Scriptures about the cross, the blood, and everything else I could use on him while I wondered what change had come to Elvis' countenance.

I found out when he began boldly rebuking Satan along with me as he too quoted several scriptural examples and oft-repeated phrases of, "Get thee behind me, Satan." He quoted them, I claimed them and then quoted some of my own!

When our prayers came to an end, Elvis looked at me, shook his head in astonishment, and with a radiant expression exclaimed, "Whew! Man, that was just like magic!" Grappling for more words he continued, "I mean every single word of it! Mary Ann, if you knew or if you even had any way of knowing . . . or . . . or . . . if you could find out the things that are going wrong in my life right now, there would be *absolutely* no way you could have prayed any better. No possible way at all. It was amazing. It was just perfect," he concluded as he fell back in his chair astounded by the accuracy of the prayers.

I was pleased by Elvis' enthusiastic reply. However, it wasn't me. It was the Lord, I explained.

Hal had been standing by the vanity with one hand raised and the other one on Elvis' shoulder while we prayed. He nervously reached for my arm at the first pause stating hurriedly, "Okay, you prayed with him. Now let's go."

I nearly fell over! What did he mean—go? I had just started!

Elvis immediately reflected a grin at the way I'd looked at Hal. "She's looking at you like I'm thinking. This is just fine. No, man, let her be. You know . . . don't worry about it!" he instructed with an increasingly edgy tone. "She's okay. She knows what she's doing man. Let her be."

"Thank you," I added as Elvis turned toward the vanity.

After picking up a book he began telling me how upset, lonely and depressed he was. I glanced at the cover. It was a study book on NUMEROLOGY.

"I consider myself a number eight person," he shared. "And

they suffer."

I became so angry at Satan and his tricks, including NUMER-OLOGY, that I knew I had to warn Elvis.

"Okay, Elvis. Okay. If you're a number eight person, then I'm a number seven person," I reasoned.

Elvis looked quickly toward Hal and then to me with widened eyes exclaiming, "That's God's number!"

"I know," I calmly replied. "And I belong to God. So I'm a number seven person too. That is if you really want to compare numbers. Another thing I must say, I'll agree 100 percent with everything in that book of yours and go home and eat or burn, at your preference, every Bible and book on Christianity that I own, if you can show me the Bible doctrine of salvation by the shed blood of Jesus Christ anywhere in the Numerology book!"

Elvis slowly turned his chair toward the vanity, took the book in his hands and began turning the first pages slugglishly. With a lingering sigh he quickly flipped the remaining pages and threw it down in disgust. After several moments of concentration he swung his chair back toward me and asked, "You're not judging me, are you?"

"No, Elvis, you know I'm not judging you. I'm judging that book by the only Book. And it's wrong, Elvis, it's wrong, it's wrong," I emphasized.

"I have moods. Don't you?" Elvis added after a lull in the conversation. "I mean sometimes I can just sit there and snarl at what I see in the mirror and other times I grin at myself like a Cheshire cat."

"Sure, I have moods too," I answered.

Hal immediately interrupted suggesting, "Let's . . ."

Elvis began shaking his head demanding, "No! No! No! Not yet. We want to talk this whole thing over." Then turning to me asked, "Don't we?"

"We certainly do," I added.

"He talks to me sometimes you know," Elvis said, pointing upward.

"Praise the Lord," I responded, knowing he meant Jesus.

With a widening grin he added, "Yes, praise God. I sure like the way you say that. You can tell when someone means it. Sometimes it's just flat. You know, nothing to it."

Offering me his chair he suggested, "Let's talk about what's going on."

"Fine with me," I cautioned with a stern expression. "But

first, you sit down and forget that you're Elvis Presley for awhile, and you prepare to be reprimanded for a change."

Smiling approvingly, he shrugged his shoulders, sat down and asked, "It's been about three and a half years now, hasn't it?"

"Yes, almost," I answered, startled by his accurate estimation of the months I'd been praying for him.

"Yeah, and don't you ever think that I haven't felt it either!" he interjected in wide-eyed confirmation, "And I mean *every single day* of it!"

As he watched to make sure all of his words had penetrated, I explained, "Well, that was the whole idea of praying daily, Elvis. So you could feel it daily."

"What do you think about the vast amounts of money that preachers are collecting? Do you think they could be hoarding it?" he questioned. "Because I know it comes mostly from people that can't really afford it."

"Well, it will take vast sums of wealth in order to fulfill the Great Commission given in Matthew 28:18-19. Maybe we all need to adjust to that," I answered.

"Yeah, you're probably right," he concluded.

Hal and Len were arguing about giving anything. Turning to them Elvis explained, "Will you stop debating the issue? If it takes these ten and twenty dollar a month offerings to get the job done, then God will repay it. And He'll build His kingdom with it. That's not for you to question."

"I was in Memphis in August of 1975 when you were sick. The Lord sent me to the hospital chapel to pray for you," I recalled.

"Yes, I know when you were there, ' he confidently stated, "and exactly when you were praying for me. It helped me tremendously. The prayers were answered, let me assure you of that.

"There were also some pictures taken of you in Memphis. I don't know how the guys did it, but anyway, they took pictures of you. I'm glad you came. I appreciated it more than I can ever show you."

"Several weeks before your hospital stay the Lord asked me to fast for three weeks and told me you would cancel out after a short time at the Hilton. On one of those days I fasted, He allowed me to see 'death,' " I slowly reflected. "I came because I was afraid you might die."

Quickly turning, he looked very knowingly adding, "Three

weeks? Without food? And He told you what might happen. For me?"

"Yes, but it was because God loves you. That's why He asked me to do all those things," I explained.

The Lord began requesting me to tell Elvis I'd been called into an evangelistic ministry. I hesitated because the ministry was in its earliest stages of confirmation. But the Lord wouldn't take no for an answer! Slowly glancing up I said, "Elvis, . . . uh . . . I . . I have a call to be an evangelist."

"I already knew that," he confidently replied, "I knew that the very first time I ever saw you. I can tell just by looking at you."

"You knew the first time you saw me?" I asked. "When was that?"

"That is my secret," he emphasized before seriously adding, "and you know, when I looked out into the other room a little while ago. Listen, nobody had to tell me which one was you. I recognized you immediately. Just as soon as I saw your face. I knew it was you."

"Elvis?" I inquired, wondering whether he or I knew the most!

"What? What do you want?" he asked, coming out of deep thought.

"Do you know that *you're* called?" I carefully asked.

"Yep," he quickly answered without a second thought or a startled reaction.

"Good," I added, "at least that will simplify things."

He became increasingly uncomfortable at the subject I had brought up. "Don't you think if I was called that God would have told me?" he asked with a mischievous expression.

"Oh, good grief, Elvis!" I added in disgust, "He did! Besides, you just admitted it. And God would not let me walk in and drop a bomb like that unless He had made it clear to you first."

"Oh . . . hum . . . didn't work," he muttered while wringing his hands.

"Well, so you know I'm called . . . huh," he considered.

After a pause he asked, "What do you think I'd preach?"

My expression immediately translated astonishment at his request.

"What kind of a preacher do you think I would be?" he requested in a gentler tone.

"You mean," I replied assessing the impossibility of his

request, "*you* want *me* to tell *you* what the Lord would want you to tell people? How you would minister to them?"

"Yes, exactly," he stated in a calm confident manner, "tell me."

Again I found myself void of the necessary information and dependent upon God for every word.

"I sense that the Lord Jesus would want you to tell them about the kind of God *you* would like to become better acquainted with and closer to. A God of compassion and love. Not a condemning God, but a saving One. I believe that is what you would preach," I answered, realizing my tempo was increasing.

And with a broken voice I continued, "There would be many people healed as you ministered and many more would be filled with the Holy Ghost and fire."

Elvis seemed to be affected by the Lord's presence again as misty-eyed, he slowly nodded his head in total agreement adding, "You've been talking to the Lord. Yes, that's *exactly* right. That's what I have felt, too."

Nevertheless, within seconds he was on his feet pacing the length of the room. As he walked he named various reasons and excuses why he couldn't preach. But as his pace quickened, his words slowly changed to perfectly quoted Scriptures, complete with an anointing of the Holy Spirit. The heavier the anointing, the faster he moved.

I became engrossed at watching his obvious reaction to God's power. But my understanding of Elvis' predicament only irritated him more. It was so very obvious that he could become quite an evangelist, if he'd only do it.

After several more trips back and forth, with increasing intensity, Elvis stopped and bent over shaking his finger in my face while loudly demanding, "What do you want, Mary Ann? What do you want? Do you want dates, too?" (referring to preaching).

"Yes, sir," I firmly responded, "I sure do. Write them down and then I can keep better track of you!"

11

HIS PERFECT WILL

Elvis shook his head in surrender, threw his hands into the air and sat down questioning, "I sing Gospel songs. Ain't that enough?"

"Nope. Not if you know you're supposed to be doing more," I affirmed. "And you know."

His uneasiness was apparent as he began fidgeting nervously.

In defense, Len quickly inserted, "There was a preacher that told Elvis that he was doing a work . . . to keep it up. What about that?"

"He did WHAT?" I demanded, nearly falling out of my chair in shock.

Elvis nodded approval at my response while Hal continued the conversation, "Yeah, he told Elvis to go on with what he was doing and sing Gospel songs. Because he was doing a work."

"Yep, he's definitely doing a work," I commented, glancing at Elvis. "Mainly on himself!"

Len kept stressing the importance of *who* it was that had told Elvis these things.

"God didn't send me out here to place one name above another," I countered, "God's Word says He doesn't delegate one man above another and I have to obey that Word. I don't care what his name is. He'll have to answer to God for his words, as well as I will for mine, and you will for yours. I'm not really worried about him anyway, it's Elvis' well-being I'm concerned about, and he can't stand in front of God on Judgment Day and point down a long line of people to whoever it was and say, 'But he said it was all right!' It doesn't work that way. It's what God says that counts."

"There are people that we get reports from," Len argued, "the word filters back to us about different ones going to Elvis' concerts and saying, 'Hey that's Elvis Presley. That no good rock-and-roll singer, and he's actually up there singing about God. Maybe we'd better find out what this is all about!' Then they go to church and get saved."

I agreed with them, because I'd felt God's presence at that concert in 1971 when Elvis sang "How Great Thou Art," and if there had been an altar I would probably have accepted Christ as my Saviour. But God doesn't sacrifice one person's happiness for another's. So why did Elvis have to remain trapped, unhappy, and sick in order to indirectly point a scattered few to God, when he could direct literally thousands and be content at the same time? It just didn't make sense as far as the way God works, and I told them so.

"See, I know most of those people who come hear me sing aren't Christians," Elvis nervously added, "So I talk about God in secret. Just between you and me. You see, it's not anyone else's business what I really believe."

I reminded him of an obligation to God and to the audience.

He responded with a silent soul-searching gaze.

"You see, if Elvis were to quit and come out completely for God . . . 100 percent . . . no one would come to hear him any longer. He couldn't draw a crowd of fifty people!" Len contended.

As I glanced toward Elvis for his response, he added, "You see, I don't think anyone would understand me. Not if I did that now. *Not now.* I just sing a song or two about God and leave it at that. To be honest, I don't think they would accept me as anything else."

"But, Elvis, you're limiting God. Do you have any idea at all what sway your name alone has? The people out there love you! They'll at least listen to what you have to say," I pleaded. "I can assure you that there are more people for you than are against you. I know, Elvis. Because I came from out there."

"I just don't see how I can preach. Not now. They'd never listen to me," he replied.

"But, Elvis, you have a call from God and an obligation with that call. You must tell them. They love you Elvis, and they would listen," I desperately reasoned.

"No, that's the problem. I don't know," he added in a fading voice.

"See those jumpsuits hanging in that closet? Forget them. And your voice and your money. They don't matter to God or to me. It's the man inside. I came because you're a man who has problems and that's where God wants to help you," I stated.

Len was still arguing with me and I interrupted asking, "Do you realize who you're talking about? I hate to be the one to have to tell you. But this is Elvis Presley . . . and he draws thousands nightly with merely the mention of his name. Add God's presence and it won't take away, it'll only double and triple. Face the facts for once, you'd have problems finding a place big enough to hold all the people."

Elvis had been listening and was agreeing with me, now.

Hal tried to get my attention as I talked to Elvis. He was becoming angry because I repeatedly disagreed with him.

"You know, you never would have had to do without or live in poverty if you would have only waited on God," I offered. "He had everything all planned for you . . . if you just hadn't jumped so soon. You're really living beneath your privileges. Regardless of what you have."

Hal tried to interrupt our conversation again. I turned to him jokingly explaining, "Be still. Can't you see I'm getting Elvis under conviction for not preaching?"

I glanced up and pointed toward Elvis, he was nodding his head affirmatively and grinning from ear-to-ear.

Hal was furious at being ignored and reached over and slapped me. Where his ring hit my forehead an immediate bruise appeared.

I couldn't believe Hal would do something like that. My feelings were hurt more than anything else and a torrent of tears followed.

Trembling, Elvis patted his gun and yelled, "You leave her alone! I don't want to ever see anything like that happen again. Do you understand me? You are to leave her alone. Don't touch her."

Then with an entirely different tone, Elvis turned and began comforting me. With a reassuring voice he whispered, "Shhh . . . it's okay. Don't cry. It's all right, don't cry. Please. Don't cry anymore. Everything is okay. He won't ever hurt you again."

I dried my eyes and looked at Hal. He was white as a sheet.

Lightening the conversation, Elvis added, "Aw, he really didn't mean to hurt you anyway."

Then abruptly turning to Hal he angrily demanded, "Did you?"

"No," Hal nervously replied, "I didn't mean to hurt her."

"Okay. What would happen to my singing?" he asked.

"I imagine God would use it. Don't you?" I replied, "but regardless, the choice will have to be His."

"You know, Mary Ann. It wasn't an accident that you were out here tonight," he confided. "This meeting was supposed to have been. Sort of destiny . . . you know what I mean? It wasn't just a coincidence. God meant it just this way."

"Yes, I know," I slowly replied. "I don't think it could have been avoided. At least, not by me anyway. Not if I really wanted to follow God . . . because this is where He led me.

"I can sympathize with you about being called," I added. "I'd much rather do small things than fly to Las Vegas. But I have to obey God, and Elvis, you will too if you want His perfect will in your life. You see, He has a permissive will as well as a perfect will."

"What's that? I've never heard of that," Elvis quickly asked. "Will you explain it to me?"

"The difference is what the Lord wants from you and what He permits you to do. His perfect will is knowing that you're doing exactly what He wants and His permissive will is doing part . . . just enough to get by and still retain His favor," I carefully explained.

After I finished talking, Elvis dropped into deep concentration, and I turned to discuss something else with Hal.

Meanwhile, Elvis had become more curious and soon interrupted, asking, "Uh . . . this permissive will you were talking about earlier. Explain more of it to me. I'm very interested."

"It's a lot like the children of Israel, Elvis, when they wanted a king . . . like all the other nations. They already knew what God *really* expected from them, because He'd made His will known. And they were held accountable for that, just like we are. Although, they knew His will, they continued to clamor for a king 'like everyone else.' So He 'gave them one in His anger' is what the Bible says. It worked for awhile. It always does. But then it fell apart, because it simply wasn't what the Lord knew would be best for them.

"That's just like us. We may want a certain thing in this life and we hound the Lord for it repeatedly. When all the time we know that it's not what He wants for us. Sometimes He'll step back and allow us to have our own way, along with all the difficulties that result from such a move."

Lowering his head, Elvis slowly replied, "I think I'm understanding things better."

After several minutes of dead silence, he changed the subject by asking, "You know how I used to run down the aisle at church and try to sing when I was just two?"

"Yeah," I added, recalling the story I'd read years ago.

"Well, I'd try to say hallelujah after I got there," he said, bursting into laughter. "Do you know how it usually came out?"

"No," I replied, finding myself laughing too.

"Something like add-gee-whoo-gee!" he replied through his hysteria.

"You should have been across the hall tonight," I added. "You would have enjoyed yourself. You should get out more often."

"Yeah," he sheepishly inquired, "what happened?"

"Lots of things. But there was a message and an interpretation. It's probably been a long time since you've heard one hasn't it?" I asked.

He nodded affirmatively and sat gazing longingly into space. "Again, you were saying something about God's will. I want to know more."

"Okay, I'll try my best," I said with an empty expression.

Cautioning me with an uplifted hand, Elvis insisted, "Now, listen. I'm really very serious about this thing you know. I really am."

As he continued reinforcing what he'd said by his expression I replied with a corresponding intensity, "I know and I've probably never been any more serious about anything in my life, either."

In answer to his question I continued, "The Lord once illustrated His perfect will to me this way. It's like being inside a whirlwind. The center is a perfect vacuum, perfectly still and calm. But when you get closer to the edge of that center you begin to be tossed around. And you keep getting tossed out further and further until you're completely gone. That's what will happen to you, Elvis, if you don't grasp a firm hold on what He wants you to do. He desires that you do what He called you to do. If you'll only submit to His calling, you can't imagine the feeling of fulfillment that it brings," I stressed.

"Yes, I know what you're telling me," he replied, closing the subject with a mutual understanding.

"Elvis," I began in response to the Lord's prompting to explain the New Year's Eve incident, "you're either going to shoot me or die laughing when I tell you this. There's no in-between to it."

"Just one way or another, huh?" he remarked.

"That's the way it looks to me anyway," I exclaimed, glancing at the gun he was carrying. "Do you remember the last New Year's Eve concert in Pontiac . . . uh . . . uh . . ." I couldn't seem to remember the state!

"Michigan?" he queried, with a grin.

"Yes, Pontiac, Michigan. Well, you see, it's like this. I wanted to know if the Lord was really hearing my prayers for you, and just how quickly He was answering them. So I asked Him to do something different on that particular night. Do you remember during the show when you. . . ." Before I could add "ripped your pants" he started snickering.

Elvis was nodding his head through his laughter as he managed to blurt out, "It was *you!* You did that. You prayed."

After Elvis regained his composure he said, "Well, it was a little embarrassing to rip the seat out of your pants in front of sixty thousand people. But it didn't surprise me that it was you! I had to have the back-up group sing . . . I think it was . . . 'Sweet, Sweet Spirit' while I backed off the stage to change to another outfit!"

"Now, I'll be in Philadelphia, Pennsylvania, this New Year's Eve," he laughed and added, "just try not to do a repeat performance if you could manage it."

"Oh, I won't, it's just that I wanted to know if my prayers were effective at a distance," I assured.

"They are definitely effective," he exclaimed with his hands raised in surrender.

"Oh, Elvis, it didn't really hurt you. You know how many times in concert you've said things like 'I hope this suit don't tear up.' So you are the one who actually supplied the idea," I replied.

He laughingly requested, "Just don't go prayin' no plagues on me and we'll get along all right."

"Oh, I won't do that. Besides, you're going to have it rough enough without *my* praying for anything but help," I explained.

12

WHAT IS LOVE?

Elvis registered interest over my last answer, although, instead of asking, he reacted by adding, "You know, it says in His Word, 'where two or three are gathered in my name there am I in the midst of them'. And man," he exclaimed, shaking in reaction to the Lord's presence, "is He ever here tonight."

"Yes, He's very close," I replied adding, "Do you realize that if you were the only one who would have accepted His sacrifice, Jesus would have hung on that cross anyway? While He suffered and died, I really feel that He looked down the corridors of time and saw you and me here tonight."

Emotion had silenced any answer Elvis could give.

And I began sensing that flow of God's love that surfaces only occasionally and always totally unsolicited. I questioned the source of my feelings, but the Lord assured me that it was His presence that I felt descending in literal waves.

Elvis had tears in his eyes as he sat mesmerized by the same Presence. His expression readily showed how deeply he was moved.

It was a moment that should have been shared by Elvis and God alone. But somehow the Lord allowed me to become involved in watching them reach out to each other.

If, as a Christian, you haven't had the awe-inspiring experience of God's love flowing through you toward another human being, then you have something truly extraordinary ahead of you. Because during that period of time an unselfish feeling envelops you and there's absolutely nothing but Christ's love . . . His agape love . . . ministering to that person through a human vessel.

It's the love that caused Stephen, the deacon in the Book of Acts, to cry out for the forgiveness of those who were stoning him in Jerusalem. And the borderline of the love of mankind that drove Jesus toward Calvary for our redemption.

Elvis reached to tap Hal on the knee, and with a weakened voice he whispered, "Look at her man, just look at her. She's beautiful. You know, that's really real, what she's got. That's real Christianity. That's it! That's what I want . . . what I see in her . . . that's what I want. I can even feel it . . . can't you feel it?" he asked Hal, "Come on, you can feel it too, can't you? It comes in waves, one right after another one. I can feel it, I can actually feel love. It's so peaceful . . ."

I was grasping for something to get his mind off "her" and on to God, but again, the Lord intercepted me by saying, "Just be still. Remain quiet and allow Elvis to talk. I'm doing something."

After ten minutes, that seemed more like two hours had passed, Elvis changed his expression to one of curiosity.

Breaking the silence I inquired, "What is it? What do you want to ask me?"

"May I ask one more question? Just one?" he carefully asked.

"Sure," I replied. "What is it you want to know? I'll say what I know and then we'll ask the Lord to add the rest . . . just like He's been doing."

"I've been around and I've studied and read a lot," he began slowly explaining. "I've thought over most of the things in this life. But I've never felt what I sensed here. There's something I want you to tell me . . . because I know you have the answer I need. Please . . . tell me . . . in your own words. What's love?"

My face registered a feeling of helplessness. Explain love, I thought. Sure, like explain creation.

"I mean really. I want to know," he pleaded.

I had no proper answer. None he hadn't read or heard before, so I asked the One who knew his heart and began, "Love is . . . giving . . . and giving . . . and giving more. And it's giving until you hurt, and after that it's *still* giving more. And, Elvis, love is giving until you die . . . and asking for absolutely nothing in return. That's love."

"Whew, that's beautiful," he softly reflected, "it's really past human words."

I agreed. Because the answer the Lord gave Elvis was so simple, as simple and yet complex as God's love for each of us.

"I don't want to be an 'Elmer Gantry,' " Elvis began, "I don't know what I'd do. What if I couldn't do it? I need time. I might have to give up singing. I don't know how I'd do it," he desperately reasoned.

"Hey, I understand your problems. But all you're saying is I . . . I . . . I. The Apostle Paul said that it's 'nevertheless not I, but Christ that liveth in me.' You're supposed to be dead. We're to die to ourselves and our own desires daily. God should steadily increase and we should decrease," I reminded him.

"Ouch!" he uttered with a guilty expression.

"Speaking of concerts and singing. The Lord told me at your concert in Kansas City in November 1971 that you needed Him," I explained. "You realize that we were in shock because you could walk and talk! I think I had my mouth open all the time you sang."

"Well," he said with a grin, "I had to do something to get your attention or you wouldn't be here tonight."

"But I was amazed that you were actually real. Do you see what I'm saying?" I explained.

"Yeah, and when you cut me I bleed too!" he said, pointing to several band-aids.

"No, you don't understand. You see, you were my god. I placed you above everything else. God has taught me to appreciate you as a person instead of placing you in a role that was impossible for you to fill. But Jesus is really what we're all looking for. Some of us just haven't discovered that yet. You should tell them, Elvis."

"Yeah," he softly muttered. "But how could *I* be anybody's god? I'm just a singer. How could anyone possibly look up to me like that?"

His confusion proved that he didn't understand how millions of people felt. So I left the subject for him to contemplate later.

"Elvis, why don't you just give up to the Lord for one day," I suggested. "You're still holding part interest in Elvis Presley . . . and that's holding up a lot of progress. You can't ever tell. He might throw back at you just what you give Him. He did me. And I'm sitting here living proof of it!"

He looked at me in suspicious unbelief as I continued. "Elvis, we need your help. We need all the help we can get! People are right now, seeing the dead raised, the maimed bodies are being restored, and untold numbers of healings are taking place through Christ's power. I, for one, would like to see some of that before I leave this earth. Wouldn't you?" I asked.

"I sure would!" he exclaimed, his eyes brightened with

excitement. "Hey, while we're on the subject, what do you think the Scripture means that talks about the dead being raised? Is that dead people or something else?"

"Actually it's physical. But if we're spiritually dead in our sins, we're resurrected spiritually to life in Christ," I explained. "So it could be either. Depending on which way you were presenting the text."

He nodded, replying, "Let me ask you something else. Do you think that before Jesus comes again, that *even* at a funeral, that a dead person . . . now I mean a corpse . . . already embalmed and laying in a coffin could be raised from the dead? Do you believe that could actually happen? I do."

"Well, let's put it like this. 'He's the same yesterday, today, and tomorrow.' There's nothing impossible with God. I think you'll recall the widow's son in Luke Chapter Seven. The woman was on her way to the cemetery to bury her son. But Jesus saw her and had compassion on her. He touched the bier, or coffin, and the boy was raised and delivered to his mother."

"That excites me," he anxiously replied. "Have you ever studied Revelation?"

"Yes, it's my favorite," I replied.

"Nearly mine, too," he agreed.

After a detailed discussion of the Second Coming of Christ and the Millenial period, he asked, "Do you think Christ is coming soon? Do you think He's coming quickly?"

"Everything points to it," I answered.

Then he asked something that caught me by surprise, and yet not by surprise, because it was something I was afraid he would do.

"You know, what you really need now is someone to stand behind you. Help you financially," he offered, looking expectantly as he talked. "Help you get started in the ministry, give you assistance . . . get you known . . . let people know you're intelligent and that you know what you're doing."

I had to refuse him for several reasons. So I cautiously replied, "Oh, Elvis. I'm sorry. But you see I already have Someone backing me."

Lowering his head in disappointment then slowly added in a sinking voice, "Oh, I didn't realize there was someone else."

To his obvious bewilderment, I smiled while adding, "Yes, there is. And if He thinks I need something more, then He'll simply stroll out on one of those thousand hills of His and sell one of those cows like He promises in His Word, Psalm 50:10."

"Oh. Okay. I see," he said with a pleased smile and an approving nod. "I see."

"It's not that I want to turn you down or hurt your feelings. But you see, I'd be cheating myself out of some valuable lessons that might be even more difficult to learn further down the line. So I have to do it His way. Do you understand? Thanks for the fantastic offer. But I have to refuse," I explained.

"I understand perfectly," he replied, changing the topic of conversation.

We began discussing Gospel music. Some of the songs we enjoyed.

"There is a story I want to share with you. It's the basis for a gospel song that's one of my favorites. May I tell you?" he inquired.

"Sure," I answered.

Shifting to the edge of his chair, he began explaining, "It seems that there was this lady in Texas, sitting in her home looking out her back door. She watched as a storm was forming out over the vast stretches of flatland. Down south, where I'm from, in Tennessee and Mississippi, the storms come up before you know they're there. Just zap and there they are. Well, anyway, she watched this storm form and a tornado dropped down from it. You know what they are, since you're from Oklahoma," he added and paused.

He even knew that! No one around him had known where I was from . . . unless they checked.

As Elvis continued explaining, he began emphasizing each word. "It began moving across the prairie, right toward the little town where she lived. Now, it could have veered off in a different direction. But listen very carefully to me. It didn't. It came right toward the town. Now you see, it didn't hit her house. And she wasn't hurt. But there were lives lost and a lot of damage was done. As she watched the power and great force behind those tremendous clouds, she was inspired to sit down and write. That's something I felt I had to share."

"It's quite a story," I tearfully remarked wondering what significance it could have for me. I've never written anything! But still, his mannerisms as he told it emphasized that I should remember every word.

Reaching to wipe a tear from my face, he examined it for awhile before explaining, "You know it's good to hurt. That's good for you to cry. Because the deeper you are allowed to feel pain and the deeper you hurt and are hurt, then the more joy you're capable of feeling afterwards. It'll help you to mature more and more as time goes by. You'll see much more happiness because of enduring more pain. You don't understand me right now. But in time you'll see what I've said is true. So please don't be sad. Be more positive about things. He'll work it all out for the good."

Quietly lowering his head, Elvis hesitated before slowly looking up to tensely request, "Mary Ann, have you ever seen the 'Ten Commandments'?"

"Yes," I answered.

"Well, do you remember the part where Moses came back down the mountain?" he asked while nervously wringing his hands.

"Yes, I remember that part."

"I mean the part where his face was lit up and shining with God's glory . . . and everyone knew that he had been with God."

"Yes," I again assured him.

"Yeah . . . yeah . . . that's it . . . that's definitely it . . ," he mumbled repeatedly.

Then glancing back toward me and motioning with his hands out from his face like sun rays he added, "Yes, uh, well, that's exactly the way you look to me. Everytime I look at you and everytime I have ever seen you. That's it. It's almost like that burning bush experience when Moses took off his shoes because he was on holy ground."

I reached to mimic taking off my shoe and we both stumbled to quote a Scripture relating the experience at the burning bush.

"Do you have a Bible here?" I asked.

"No, I don't think so," he said, looking around the room.

"Have you ever seen a Dake's Bible?" I asked.

"No. What's that?" he eagerly asked.

"It's a study and reference Bible equivalent to several volumes," I explained. While I continued his face lit up like a child's at his first Christmas. Now what do I say, when it's obvious he wants one . . . and yet he could buy all that had ever been published?

"Would you like to have one?" I inquired. "Would you read it?"

"Would I? Really? You mean it? Yeah, sure I'd like that. That's great," he enthusiastically replied.

"Okay, when I get back home, I'll buy one for you. And I brought a book of poems to you. Christian poetry. I know you've always had a preference for poems. It's over in my room, but I'll get it to you before I leave Vegas," I concluded.

"You brought me poetry? What don't you know about me?" he asked with a chuckle.

"Lots of things, Elvis. I only know what God tells me so I can pray for you," I answered. "But there is one more thing I want you to remember, if you don't remember another word that was spoken here tonight."

"What's that?" he interjected.

"No matter where you are or what you're doing you can rest assured that not a day passes by that I haven't spent at least an hour on my knees praying specifically for you."

"I'll remember you're there. But that's something I've known for quite sometime. It's helped me alot to know you're praying. Tell me, are there any perfect Christians out there?" he asked.

"No, not that I know of. We're not perfect, we're just forgiven and trying!" I assured him. "There's just one perfect One that I know anything about."

"Jesus, right?" he inquired.

"Right!" I added.

"Do me one more favor, will you?"

"What?" I asked.

"Just wait," he replied with a patient expression. "Just wait. Just wait. This thing is going to work out all right. But it takes time. It's taken me seventeen years to just learn to wait on God. And this is going to be fine. It'll work out. I promise you faithfully that everything will be just perfect."

I had to smile as the dream where Elvis had asked me to read James 5:10 flashed through my mind.

"Yes, I know it takes time and we have to wait," I told him. "But please don't wait too long . . . you don't have that kind of time."

Shaking my finger at him, I further cautioned, "Elvis, the Lord and I are going to get you . . . one way or the other."

"Well," he sighed, slumping into his chair. "You just might, you just might."

"Elvis, seriously, are there two guys after you?" I asked, wondering about the rumored book.

Without looking up, he slowly nodded his head affirmatively.

I wanted to ask if the stories were true. But before I could, the Lord requested that I not intrude.

"After all," He asked, "what difference does it make now?"

None, I thought. *None.*

13

YOU BETTER RUN

Hal was called out of the room to talk to the bodyguards who were anxious to leave.

After Hal left, Elvis sent Len out for refreshments, and I realized my request to talk privately with him had been granted.

"Are you going to make it, Elvis? Will everything be all right?" I pleadingly questioned him. "It's got to. You've just got to make it."

He lowered his head and considered my questions before answering, "Yes, I promise you that it'll be fine. I promise. I'll get this thing together."

"You're sure then?" I implored.

"Hey, I promised you didn't I?" he confidently replied. "After all, where would I be now if you hadn't been praying?"

Nearly an hour later, after Elvis had given me a standing invitation to any back stage areas wherever he was and had insisted that I have a lightning-bolt necklace like he gave his closest friends, he stood up to leave.

"Well, I'm not going to say good-by. That's too final. Besides, I'll see you again," I explained.

"Yeah, you know you will," he quickly affirmed. "You know you will."

Then gently leaning over, he laid his head on my shoulder and began trembling.

"Elvis, don't you know?" I whispered.

"Yeah, I do," he replied in a quiet voice as he raised his head.

After a moment of intense stillness he turned to walk away.

Hal, Len and I walked out behind Elvis. The outer room was emptied now.

As I found myself wondering when everyone had left, Len and Hal suddenly appeared in front of me shaking their fingers in my face informing me in no uncertain terms to stop trying to change Elvis.

"What if you'd change him and he's lose all of his popularity?" they both demanded angrily. "What if you would ruin him? You wouldn't want that. What if no one would listen to him? He couldn't change now, he's too old. He's doing fine like he is, leave him alone."

Their anger subsided when I explained that I couldn't change anybody.

Overlooking the fact that God can, they accepted my answers.

The three of us walked back through hallways and elevators to reach the twenty-first floor. Before I stepped onto the public elevators to leave them, I called to Hal, "Thanks for your help."

With a self-conscious expression, Hal stopped and quickly turned to me, stating, "Hey! I didn't get you in, he did," as he pointed to Elvis' suite.

On the way to the lobby, the Lord took advantage of my first quiet moments by very graciously saying, "Thank you for taking Me in with you."

"You got it, Lord!" I exclaimed as I headed for the phones in the lobby to call home.

I seriously doubt if anyone else had ever run through the downstairs of the Las Vegas Hilton proclaiming, "Glory to God, Thank You, Jesus!" But early that morning I did! I sure did!

From a half-closed phone booth I dialed Jerry. When he answered I began exuberantly explaining, "I just spent three hours with Elvis. We talked about God and prayed together. And he wants a Dake's Reference Bible!"

I don't remember Jerry getting in any other words but "Hello!"

I walked back to the Landmark before calling Denise long enough to turn her into a shouting Methodist!

Daybreak came before I could rest. Calling the night lost, I made plans to find Elvis' Bible in Vegas.

I randomly picked a name out of the phone book and dialed the Christian Supply Center to ask if they stocked them. And they did.

So I phoned Trinity Temple, explaining my position and asked if a member of the staff could drive me to the bookstore. But, before Assistant Pastor Gebhart took me to buy it, the phone rang.

It was one of the girls that had been in the dressing room the night before, asking, "Did you see Elvis?"

"Yes, for several hours," I replied.

"It was near morning before my girl friend and I could get out of the restaurant. We were with two of Elvis' friends. And people kept coming over to our booth asking all sorts of questions," she spontaneously exclaimed. "Things like, 'What went on down there?', 'Where did she come from?', and 'Who was that little gal down there gettin' into everybody's minds? One of the guys we were with mentioned that there were a lot of big people to buck, but the job was getting done anyway."

Later that evening I went back to the Hilton with Elvis' Bible for Hal to see.

After glancing through it he demanded, "Open it and write."

The message he persuaded me to write was long and personally encouraging. Included was the statement "I'll see you in Heaven," with a simple salutation of "Peace."

I realized that giving Elvis a Bible wasn't a new invention. But his being excited over wanting one and the Lord supplying it was a different subject entirely.

"Was Elvis serious last night or was he 'snowing' me?" I asked, needing confirmation from Hal.

"Elvis wasn't 'snowing' you," he answered with a stunned expression, "He doesn't have to 'snow' anybody. He could have signalled to me and we'd have dragged you out. And it wouldn't have been the first time that would have happened. That's why I kept saying, 'We'd better go.' You couldn't have known what he was doing, but he kept telling me he wanted you to stay. He enjoyed your company."

"But how long will he remember what was said?" I questioned.

He sighed, shook his head, and answered, "Just let me tell you this much. And then you can figure out the rest. I know Elvis and I know him well enough to know that even if he tried to forget you, or what you said to him last night, he couldn't. Not even if he did nothing else *but that* until the day he died. There's no way he can forget. You told him the truth, and what's more he knew it. I've been with everyone who has ever talked to him in this way, and no one has ever reached him the way you did. Do you hear me, *no one!*

"You helped him tremendously. What more do you want? A new-born baby doesn't get up and run first. They crawl for awhile. No, you don't have to worry about Elvis forgetting what you said. He can't!"

A more thorough answer I've never received! Or, for that matter, a more welcome one.

Again that evening, I went with Hal to the dressing rooms.

That night Elvis requested several members of the group to sing Gospel numbers that had the audience clapping in tempo.

Several statements were made proving that he had been doing some deep thinking. Walking across the stage with a limp, caused by an injured leg, he paused and remarked, "What a mess, man. This image for twenty-one years now. I must be crazy."

Hal's girl friend and a girl from Sacramento were also in the dressing room. After one of Elvis' sultry remarks about his career, Hal's girl friend turned to me admitting, "You must have really gotten to Elvis last night."

Realizing that she had observed him for sometime and would know, I answered, "Well, the entire point of coming to Las Vegas was to 'get to' Elvis."

The other girl glanced at me suspiciously while asking Hal's friend, "Why did Elvis go on so many tours in 1976? He doesn't need the money! Does he? And it's quite obvious he needs the rest."

Looking at her and then toward me, Hal's friend dramatically explained, "Money . . . does *not* buy happiness!"

During those three days, sleep was replaced by seasons of kneeling or lying face down on the floor of my room pleading with God for Elvis' ministry.

On the third day I asked the Lord for a scriptural guide to show me if I was to go to the Hilton again.

I picked up Elvis' Bible and opened it. My eyes fell on Judges 6:18, stating, "Depart not . . . until I come . . . and bring forth my present, and set it before thee. . . . I will tarry until thou come again."

Once that answer was clarified, I began praying again and immediately was shown a brown eagle with shabby ruffled feathers.

In my inability to comprehend His message, I asked the Lord for an explanation.

The memory of a molting bird I'd once seen came to my mind, and I knew that this eagle was adapting to a like change. But why an eagle? And why molting feathers?

That question was answered as the Lord led me to the Bible with the words, "Seventeen and seven."

102

Without hearing further instruction I casually opened the Bible. Again, the appropriate Scriptures awaited my glance. For, Ezekiel 17:7-8 reads, "There was another great eagle with great wings and many feathers . . . this vine did bend her roots toward him. . . . It was planted in a good soil by great waters, that it . . . might bear fruit . . ."

In the Scripture I'd seen the molting bird, that seemed to represent Elvis. The vine is Christ, as are "my roots." Planted in good soil by great waters told me that the time had been right.

I dressed and prepared to leave. As I walked out the door the Lord added, "You're going to run into someone when you get over there. But go into the restaurant first."

"Okay. But no waiting lines or I won't go," I requested.

As I had asked, there was no line. After the hostess seated me, I turned to look toward the entrance and a long line had seemingly materialized from nowhere.

After lunch I left the restaurant and the Lord led me into the gift shop.

A familiar voice caused me to turn around. There stood someone else I'd prayed for once, Liberace.

He immediately greeted me and the opportunity presented itself to tell him about the Lord, as had the opportunity to witness to several other well-known people who were normally difficult to reach.

Walking back into the lobby, I literally ran into someone— Hal!

"Oh, no. It's you!" I complained.

"What do you mean by that?" he sharply replied with a grin. "And what are you doing?"

After filling him in on the Lord's latest bulletins, I added, "If I'd known the Lord had meant I'd run into you, I don't think I'd have come back!"

"Thanks," he replied with a chuckle.

"But since I'm here, I do want to tell you that I need fifteen minutes of your time sometime today."

Glancing at his watch he asked, "Okay. How about right now?"

"Sure, if it's agreeable with you," I answered.

"Do you want her there while you're talking? Or can you talk openly in front of her?" he inquired, motioning toward his friend.

"I don't really think that's the question," I replied. "Can you talk openly in front of her? She doesn't bother me at all."

Hal let out a sigh, raised his eyebrows, looked at me and directed a statement to her. "Go get your hair fixed . . . or something. We need to talk. And I think what she has to say is going to be some pretty heavy stuff," he admitted.

As she walked away we went to talk. The welfare of his soul was first on the agenda.

While I paced the floor and explained God's plan for his life I noticed that the excuses he'd used the first three days I'd been there were no longer in use. Simply because all his questions had been answered!

"I know you realize I'm serious about all this and that it's God's moving rather than mine," I commented.

"Yes, we know," he replied continuing with the conversation. "Does this sound familiar?" he requested as he began quoting verbatum the conversation he and I'd had over three years earlier. "See I told you then that the walls would fall."

I stopped pacing long enough to listen.

"I've begged Elvis to write down or tape some of the things he knows about the Bible and God," he confided through tears, "It's deep, Mary Ann. He's good. He's really good. And I'm so afraid that he'll die or something will happen to him before he can do it."

"It will, Hal," I remorsefully recalled. "Do you remember the message the Lord left in Kansas City last April? It's going to happen. I don't know the exact date yet. But it'll happen. And when it does just remember that three-fourths of me is going to die too. You see, I know too much to remain neutral now."

That evening after I had gone with Jackie Kahane, the show comedian, Hal, and Bill Belew, Elvis' tailor, to do some charity and promotional work, I made my third trip to the backstage area. Still carrying Elvis' Bible!

Just prior to the start of the show, one of Elvis' colleagues came dashing in the door hysterically exclaiming, "Elvis has strep infection and he doesn't want to do the show."

Everyone panicked!

They collectively managed to dissuade him from his initial reluctance. Elvis was having difficulty with his leg as well, and he had no business even trying to perform. However, the show was rather short and interspersed with several Gospel songs.

Through it all, I became amused when Elvis ended "Lord, This Time You Gave Me a Mountain" and moaned before adding, "Ugh! Well, somebody did!"

The close of the concert interrupted tradition.

Elvis surveyed the audience and stated, "Now there's something I want to do before I leave here. Because I've never done this before and I've always had a hankerin' to do it . . . if you don't mind. I may never be seein' you for a long time, so I'd like to do a couple 'a three uh . . . spirituals for you."

After a suggestion from the audience he responded, "Naw, naw, this is something I've never done before." And with a pleased voice added, "We're fixin' to sing about Him."

After explaining to the group that he was going to begin with a fast-paced spiritual, less any orchestration he began, "You better run . . . that's what I said . . . You better run . . . when I say, Somebody's calling me up and I feel like my time ain't long . . . long."

Singing it several times he stopped and requested, "Okay . . . Rock my Soul." "Welllll . . . you rock my soul . . . ," the singer began. As the band joined in, Elvis impatiently demanded, "Whoa, whoa, whoa . . . band! *No* instruments. Now, listen to this, okay? Just listen to the words."

Then, as old-style quartet harmony is reborn on stage, the concert is brought to an early ending with an apology for his illness and a quick departure and a sincere "God Bless You."

In the basement after the show I talked with three members of the group.

"What was he doing out there tonight?" I asked.

Their unanimous answer was, "I don't know what he was doin'. He's never done anything like that before. He even changed the words to 'You Better Run.'"

After everyone had wandered away from the area, Hal looked over at me and flatly stated, "I'm not going to take him that Bible tonight. He'll probably not want to see me now anyway. But regardless, he's too sick. And I don't want him getting into anything that heavy right now. You have my gilt-edged triple-bonded guarantee that he'll get it . . . because I heard him say he wanted it!"

"Lord, Elvis needs something heavy now!" I quickly inserted. "He's thinking."

Since Hal refused to take it, I decided to keep it and go to Wichita, Kansas, on December twenty-seventh and give it to Elvis in that concert.

"Elvis needs that Bible now, tonight. And you'll *not* take it home with you!" the Lord firmly exclaimed.

"Okay," I mentally replied. "But how are You going to do that? The door just shut on us."

As the idea surfaced to ask Hal to take the poetry book to Elvis I sympathetically offered, "Well, at least take this book of poems to him. It's not too heavy. And maybe it'll help cheer him up."

Hal raised his head sternly insisting, "Okay, but I'm not going to take that book without that Bible!"

I couldn't believe his startling change. There wasn't any doubt that God had intervened.

"Well, it's fine with me," I offered. "If you're sure that it's not too much for him."

"No, I want Elvis to have them now. Go on upstairs and wait on me," Hal stated as he walked out the door. "I'll be up in a few minutes."

The clock moved as if it were made of lead until Hal came slowly walking through the door with his head lowered to conceal his emotions.

Trying to regain his composure before speaking, he sat with his head resting on his hand.

"Well . . . I gave Elvis the Bible," he began with an emotionally-torn voice. "And when he saw that Bible . . . he broke," he quickly stated, echoing Elvis' response.

"He sent you a message," he continued, "and he told me to deliver it to you personally."

"What did he want you to say to me?" I asked.

After intently concentrating on his subject, he added, "Elvis said . . . 'Tell her . . . that I love her. And tell her that no one . . . no, no one has ever cared this much . . . no, not this much.' "

Pausing again to take a firm grip on his emotions, Hal merely proved that he understood the deeper meaning of Elvis' words.

Again with a look of unbelief at what he'd been repeating, Hal continued Elvis' message. "Then he told me, 'You tell her I'll keep this Bible forever and I'll cherish it for the rest of my life. Oh, and tell her that I'll start reading it right now.' That's what he said."

I grappled for words, but none seemed appropriate. Blurting out a short incomprehensible, "Fine," I sat hiding my own tears.

Hal leaned forward in his chair sternly reinforcing the words with, "And I know Elvis . . . and just in case you have any questions. He meant every single word of it."

"Yes, I'm sure he did," I slowly answered. "I have to go now."

106

As I closed the door to the room Hal yelled, "Slow down a little and come down a few miles."

"No," I responded. "You'll have to come up where I am."

I bounced down the hall and onto the elevator. I was ready to leave Las Vegas.

Once on the airplane the next day, I glanced across the aisle to find the same couple seated there who had been across from me on the flight out.

Suddenly I remembered them as the couple working in the travel agency in a dream I'd had in preparation for coming to Vegas!

That was just another road sign from the Lord showing me I was on the right track.

Jerry picked me up at the airport and we drove home discussing what the Lord had done.

Susan called shortly after we had come in asking, "What were you doing around two in the morning last Monday?"

"I was with Elvis, why?" I quizzed.

"It seems that all I could do for over three hours was pray for you and him," was her reply.

Less than a week passed before the young evangelist who had asked prayer for Elvis before the April concert in Kansas City spoke at our church again.

After his sermon that night, an altar call was given. He requested that people carrying burdens for others come forward for prayer.

While I stood at the altar, he walked toward me, and it startled me as he was speaking words that coincided with the Scriptures that I'd received in Las Vegas. Without realizing the importance of what he was saying he began confirming Ezekiel 17:7 as he prophesied words under the anointing of the Holy Spirit.

"You have planted the seed and watered it," the Lord revealed. "It *has* taken root and it *is* growing. It will bring forth a *great* and a *vast* harvest. But just don't forget that it's God that gives the increase."

Denise turned into a shoutin' Methodist for the second time in a week and Kate, another friend who had helped me pray for Elvis, registered pure satisfaction that the Lord had provided.

"That was for me . . . I just came back from Vegas," I told the evangelist after services. "Mission accomplished! Every prayer, every tear, every night of walking the floor and worrying, every moment of my frustrations . . . it was worth every bit of it!"

14

THE VISION FULFILLED

A formal invitation dated May 5, 1977, requesting my presence at a concert by Elvis in Kansas City formed the main emphasis of a dream the Lord had given me in answer to my plea to know when I'd see Elvis again.

On the third day of March, the Lord led me aside and asked two questions that I assumed were only incidental.

"Don't you think Elvis is doing what I had planned right now . . . today?" the Lord inquired.

Then turning to another point He asked, "Do you think this is all climaxing?"

The only answer I could give was, Yes, or step directly into unbelief.

The reason for the questions being asked on that particular day came to my attention several weeks after Elvis' death when they probated his will, dated March 3, 1977!

The Imperials Quartet, a group that had once sung behind Elvis, appeared in Kansas City in April.

During the past few years I'd become acquainted with them and had confided to one member of the group that I was praying for Elvis.

As I entered the auditorium I called to him, "I went to Las Vegas in December."

"Oh, yeah? And what's his name?" he smiled before quickly running to me.

"Elvis?" I slowly answered.

"Elvis Presley!" he exclaimed.

"Shhh, not so loud," I said, looking around at the people who had stopped to listen. "Do you want to start a riot?"

"Hey, will you tell the other guys after the concert that you prayed with Elvis? It would bless them tremendously," he said.

"Sure," I replied.

At the close of the evening I shared my feelings and fears with Jim and Armond. With tear-filled eyes we joined hands and prayed for Elvis before I left.

Still more visionary guidance surfaced at the close of March. I found myself in a prayer meeting, listening to a lady giving forth a prophecy. Listening, although not applying what she was saying, even though the message related an ending to something that had taken a process of years to accomplish.

Pointing toward me, she continued the prophecy relating, "What makes you think this isn't for you? In the month that hastens to begin (April), it will begin to be fulfilled."

My thoughts backtracked to the Hilton Inn on April 21, 1976, when I had told Hal that Elvis had a year to live.

Another of Elvis' ex-travelling companions, who is now working for the Lord full time, came through Kansas City. That evening after he had spoken, we renewed an old friendship and talked about Elvis. Before parting, we joined hands and prayed for Elvis, asking God to bring him to a full knowledge of what he was to do.

The following morning I read a news release reporting that Elvis had cancelled his concert in Baton Rouge at the exact time we had been praying.

Morning found Elvis back at Baptist Memorial Hospital in Memphis.

During April I was shown another vision. This time the Lord was standing with His shepherd's crook in hand, while He looked patiently toward the ground. As my mind registered curiosity, I was allowed to see a ram trapped deep in the thicket of a bush. With his horns interlocked, the ram struggled and shook his head while pawing the ground viciously as it struggled to escape. But to no avail.

As the scriptural reference came to mind the Lord answered my unasked questions explaining, "Yes, Christ is the sacrifice. But here it represents Elvis' struggling. And I have provided a sacrifice for him. But he will escape at the very last minute."

"Have you heard the latest about Elvis?" Denise's husband, Jerry, asked as I answered the door a few days later.

"No, what?"

"Just wondered," he said, walking away.

After Denise and I dragged him in the house he proclaimed, "All I heard was that Elvis is coming back to Kansas City in June."

Suddenly I realized this was May 5, 1977, just like on the invitation I'd seen.

Denise and I left at four A.M. the morning that tickets went on sale anticipating a quick depletion of seats like on previous occasions.

But this time they didn't sell out until the afternoon of the concert nearly two months later.

We talked with two fans and discovered they had been in Las Vegas when I was there.

The day of his performance arrived quietly. If you can call praying twenty-four hours a day and walking the floor all night as being quiet!

Several days before the concert, a picture of the arena where Elvis was scheduled to perform appeared in the paper.

The effect was staggering as I read the caption "Storm Warning" and glanced at the jagged lightning bolt that seemingly pierced the white building.

On June 18, 1977, the date of the concert, Jerry, Denise, Jerry and I found our seats at the arena early.

Denise and I left to find Hal, but instead, found the two girls we'd met in the ticket line.

"We've been looking all over for you," exclaimed one of them. "Ever since we came here we've been going from door to door asking the ushers if they had seen a black-haired girl come through."

"Well, at least we found each other," I said, glancing at another girl that was with them this time and remembering a Scripture the Lord had given me earlier in the day concerning three people that would be seeking me.

"You know Elvis, right?" the new girl questioned.

"Yes."

"Well, could it be true? I mean I've heard . . . could he have . . . there's rumors. . . . Well, you're a Christian," she nervously implored, "could it be that Elvis became a Christian about six and a half months ago? Is that true? Could that be right?"

Denise and I looked at each other in shock! We hadn't told a soul.

"Let's just put it this way," I began, "I did buy Elvis a Bible . . . because he wanted it. So let's say it's very probable that he made such a decision to do that."

110

All three of them breathed a sigh of relief. "When you talk to him tell him how thrilled we are that he's found happiness at last. Will you?"

"Sure, but why don't you write him a note and I'll put it in the *Bible Handbook* I brought for him. Then he can read it for himself," I offered.

They hastily wrote a note, signed it, and placed it in the book for Elvis.

Joe Guercio, Elvis' orchestra conductor, was standing nearby.

"Where's Hal?" I inquired.

"Backstage. He'll be out soon. How are you?" he called.

"Fine. Tell Hal I want to talk to him."

When Hal walked out I bluntly asked if I could see Elvis, knowing the answer to such a question before I asked.

"Nope," he replied bluntly. "There's no way!"

"Oh, I see." I replied remembering the exact response from June, 1974. "I brought him a book . . . can I get it to him?"

"No," came his cold dead reply.

"I see," I added, slowly walking away.

Denise, the three girls and I left to find our seats before the concert started.

As we walked down the hall they began asking questions. After I'd run out of answers, I asked the Lord what I could tell one of the girls.

Stopping in the hall I sighed, "Okay, look! I'm going to Bible School. Hopefully to one day be an evangelist. And I did pray with Elvis. The Lord sent me to Las Vegas."

Bouncing around she began exclaiming, "I knew it! I knew it!"

I glanced at Denise in bewilderment. It was as if they had been waiting for my admission.

During the beginning of the concert I was sitting near an aisle close to the stage as the orchestra played the introduction.

Elvis slowly walked out and was physically assisted onto the stage. "Oh, God," I cried. "How much further down can he go? He can't even stand up alone!" My mind raced to compare the physical deterioration of just the past six months' time. It was obvious that he couldn't continue much longer.

As he sang the first song, I walked up to one of the guards asking, "Is it possible to approach the stage?"

"The security has been tightened for tonight," he explained, glancing at the book in my hands.

"Oh, I can't get the book to him," I sighed realizing that Elvis wasn't aware of my presence for the first time since I'd begun praying.

"I'll take the book to him," he softly replied.

As he reached for the volume in my hands, I looked at Elvis fearfully explaining, "He's dying, you know."

"No, ma'am, I don't know," he reflected, pausing a moment to turn toward the stage. "But it could very well be."

Walking back to my seat was the longest walk I've ever taken. Stopping long enough to talk to one of the other guitar players I mumbled, "It doesn't look good, does it?"

With a dread in his eyes, he shrugged his shoulders and slowly looked at Elvis. He couldn't even remember the words to the songs he had been singing since his career began over twenty years earlier.

Becoming physically ill, I walked into the hall and leaned against a doorway to watch the rest of the concert while my tears flowed freely.

Jerry stood in the hall shaking his head in dismay as the people walked out on Elvis' performance.

"It's out of your hands, Mary Ann," the Lord began warning. "He's going to die. It's all been done. He'll be all right . . . because I promised you. But he's going to die."

I shook my head violently, refusing to listen.

Suddenly I caught a glimpse of something blue sailing across the stage. "There goes your book," the Lord quickly assured me.

When Elvis began singing his final number, Denise and Jerry joined us in the hallway. As she and I walked down the hall she began trying to cheer me up. It was useless. I had already heard and seen too much. Time and space could not hold the emptiness I felt at that moment. Bewilderment, pain, defeat and frustration surrounded me as I wondered why.

Realizing my frustration, the Lord softly said, "Go to where the cars come out of the building."

"Let's go," I called to Denise as I remembered where the driveway to the basement was located.

Denise and I stood beside the large overhead door that led into the arena. As it opened I saw Hal sitting in the front of the first car.

When he saw me standing there, he quickly reached to tap someone on the knee.

As I followed his movements I saw Elvis.

Hal began violently pointing toward me after receiving his attention. Elvis casually turned to observe what Hal's frantic actions had meant.

As he saw me, a look of unearthly hope radiated from his eyes, communicating a fond remembrance.

As the limousine turned into the street Elvis' expression evolved to one of pleading. Pulling himself forward and jerking the towel from his neck when it obstructed his view he looked back in desperation.

On Elvis' request, the car rolled to a stop at the corner. Still looking back he reflected the agony of a man trying to contain the Creator within a subdued vessel.

Elvis' car had been followed by two others, causing Denise to remark, "The sound of that garage door opening and those three cars . . . I experienced that two weeks ago during prayer."

Jerry and I went to the airport the next day to tell Elvis good-by.

Although he had already communicated his appreciation for the book and my presence at the concert, I felt I should illustrate my support one more time.

As soon as we arrived at the airport, a man stepped out of his jet, walked over to me and said, "Elvis won't be leaving until six this evening."

When Elvis arrived, he hesitated a moment as he was quickly ushered up the steps to the plane. Turning to me with a knowing smile he waved the handbook at me.

As he continued walking away, I screamed through my mounting fears, "Elvis. Stop!"

Abruptly turning around at the doorway, he reflected, "I can't."

While I stood frozen with anxiety, thoughts of another airport and another time entered my mind.

After I'd begun praying for Elvis an elderly Christian lady related an incident that occurred at an early point in Elvis' career.

At the end of a week-long prayer meeting devoted mostly to praying for Elvis, he had responded by running into a church to ask for forgiveness.

Within hours, he caught a plane for the coast. When he arrived several of his associates met him threatening, "Don't you ever do that again! We'll make you wish you'd never seen us. We'll break you!"

After that incident Elvis regarded his spiritual life as separate

113

and hidden from anyone except a few close friends.

Walking up the steps to talk to Ed Parker, one of Elvis' friends, I left the same message . . . that I was praying and waiting.

I didn't bother Elvis. I knew he'd call if he wanted to talk.

As the jet taxied down the runway six familiar hands shot out of the cockpit window waving frantically. Recognizing them all . . . I finally waved . . . to the nodding acknowledgment of each one.

Elvis waving *Halley's Bible Handbook* to me when boarding his plane.

15

STORMS AHEAD

"If I take Elvis now, without him coming into a ministry, can you accept that it's best for you and this has all been My plan?" the Lord carefully asked. "That's the way you win the victory over Satan and stand on what I've promised for you."

"No," I angrily replied, while inwardly knowing I would have to.

Through a series of insurmountable problems our vacation plans were cancelled and instead we found ourselves back in Memphis again.

My pleas for a reason brought little response, other than a Scripture in Luke 19 implying a loosing of some sort.

I thought at the time that it meant Elvis coming to a decision on preaching, which would be reason enough for me to go to Tennessee. Although, every time I had talked to Elvis, this was something he had showed a great deal of unrest about.

Instead, it was me who felt the loosing. It seemed the Lord was allowing me to see Elvis one more time before He took him.

When we arrived in Memphis, I asked one of Elvis' buddies how he was.

With a concerned expression he explained, "Elvis is home. But he's very sick."

He also told us that Elvis had started walking to the gates of Graceland a few days earlier after telling the fans waiting that he'd come and answer any questions they asked. If only they would not scream.

Three-fourths of the way down the drive, some of the people yelled, Elvis stopped and shook his head in disappointment, before returning to the house to be seen by the public no more.

After we parked in front of Elvis' house, Jerry's attention was drawn toward the guardhouse. I followed his gaze to find several people straining to look across the fence at us.

As the iron gates opened, one young man walked out and focused his camera in our direction, snapped a picture and disappeared inside the gates once again.

It looked like Elvis was involved in another episode of picture-taking like he had been two years earlier when I'd visited him at Baptist Memorial Hospital.

Inquisitiveness overtook me as I sensed an urging to walk to the front gate. No sooner had I stopped when here came Charley Hodge.

As I walked over to talk to him, we clasped hands while I inquired, "How is he? How's he feeling?"

Instead of answering, he looked down. His actions told me more than his words ever could have.

"Tell Elvis hello for me and tell him I was here. I don't want to bother him. Just tell him I'm still praying and I have no intentions of quitting as long as he's still breathing," I replied.

That was July 16. Elvis was to die exactly one month later. Again Charley looked away, then with his usual grin and a wink said, "I'll tell you what. I'll tell Elvis. But you know we need the prayers and I know you need the practice."

"Okay, Charley. See you later," I replied to one of his stock answers. And left a book of Christian-centered quotes for Elvis. I left books with him every time I was near him because I knew he read books on various religions and sometimes that isn't too safe. I thought I should at least counteract some of it with Christian theology. Although Elvis wasn't alone in doing that. A lot of Christians read a lot of things that could lead to spiritual harm.

On the way to Tupelo, Mississippi, I remembered I'd wanted to visit Elvis' mother's grave at Forrest Hills Cemetery.

"Oh, well, it's not as if we'll never be back again. I'll just wait and go next time I'm in Memphis," I explained, shuddering at the thought.

When we arrived in Tupelo, the Lord led us directly to Elvis' old neighborhood. When we located the Assembly of God Church I knew I'd also located the lady I'd called and written to throughout the nearly four years of praying for Elvis. When I walked to a neighbor's house to find her, she answered the door instead. "Is that you, Mary Ann?" she asked with tears filling her eyes.

"Yes, it's me. I finally made it," I replied, hugging her as if we'd been close friends all our lives.

"How did you find me?" she asked.

"The Lord led us directly through town and here."

"Yes . . . ," she said, her knowing words fading into a smile.

After we attended night services at Elvis' boyhood church, we were introduced to everyone there and they seemed to know who I was.

"You know, Elvis got his start right here," a middle-aged native of Tupelo spontaneously explained to Jerry.

"Here?" Jerry asked.

"No, in the yellow house across the street," he answered. "God's really dealing with Elvis. You can tell that, and I for one know he's had a taste of God's power."

Later that evening after we'd returned from church we shared our lives.

Changing the subject to her sister who had recently gone to be with the Lord, she reflected, "Before she passed away she used to ask me every other day or so if you had taken your vacation yet. I'd tell her I didn't know and assured her you were praying for us. She'd answer by firmly stating that you would be here this summer, but she'd be gone before you arrived. I cautioned her about talking that way, but she persisted with her statements. Now it appears she was right."

Continuing with her conversation she added, "Whenever I mention your name or talk of you, some will ask me where I'd ever met you or if I've ever seen you before. I always tell them I haven't seen you, but you'll be here. I don't know when just yet, but when she comes I'll know her. Because one of these days she's comin' home to Tupelo . . . to us."

Misty-eyed we exchanged fixed gazes as I stood there with "coming home to us" ringing in my ears and wonderment in my mind.

I wanted to ask her why, but wisdom told me to remain silent.

Southern hospitality radiates from Tupelo as it does from all small southern towns and we were compelled to spend the night with her.

Morning came. It was hot and humid at daybreak. A day much like those I remember from my childhood in Oklahoma . . . in a neighborhood much like this one.

I found our hostess bustling around the kitchen preparing a huge breakfast for us.

"As a matter-of-fact," she assured me with a twinkle in her matronly eyes, "Elvis' favorite breakfast whenever he visits my home."

The day was spent surveying Tupelo from top to bottom with a very able guide.

Toward evening we started for Nashville and only a few miles north of Tupelo we passed Elvis heading south.

As I recognized his car, I leaned forward in my seat for a better look.

"That's Elvis!" I exclaimed to Jerry as Elvis passed us with a big smile and a familiar wave.

"Are you sure?" he asked.

"If it is he'll talk to you," I added.

Within seconds Elvis was motioning us to pull off the road. After we talked awhile, he carefully warned, "Watch out up the road. I just drove through a terrible storm. The wind is blowing and it's hailing. It's bad. So wait until it passes by before you go on."

With that we went our separate ways without any mention of a ministry. I wondered aloud if Elvis' storm might prove more personal than either of us knew at the time.

On our way back to Kansas City, Jayne Ann quizzically inquired, "Mom, when are you going back to Memphis again?"

"Oh, honey, it'll be . . . ," I began, when suddenly the words "about a month" wedged themselves into my mind. The irrational words were quickly dismissed as I continued with my originally intended, ". . . quite a while."

We hadn't been home from Tennessee more than a week when I received another vision.

This time I was alone in a boat on a vast bloody sea. My oar became lodged on something floating on the thick, crimson liquid. Reaching down to free it, I recoiled at the sight. Rather than an incidental portion of barren driftwood, the repugnant spectacle of dismembered limbs and heads of decaying humanity met my glance. Wrestling with the intense heat and thick darkness, I strained to belie stark reality, only to find this horrid scene justified itself manyfold in the distance.

Catching a shadowy glimpse of a man frantically waving his arms in an attempt to get my attention, I began hurriedly rowing toward him.

Even though everyone here was dead, he had miraculously survived. Glancing up to check my course, I was startled to discover that it was Elvis.

Although he was in a weakened condition when I helped him into the boat, he took the oars and maneuvered the lifeboat toward the only escape he could take . . . through death.

The stench of dead, decaying mortality was so strong throughout the vision that it remained with me for several days.

A dream closed the month of July. This time Jerry and I were home and both girls were outside. A strange noise caused Jerry and I to go out to observe a terrible storm boiling and churning in the southern skies. In place of thunder, the sounds imitated hideous screams of terror.

I called to warn the girls, but they were too far away to be able to hear me. Frantically turning toward the imminent storm, I desperately grabbed my ears shrieking, "Oh, God, no! It can't be." As my hysteria subsided into emotional deadness, I calmly surveyed the neighborhood. Everyone was standing outside staring as if they were mechanical robots. Although I only saw a few people, I sensed that they had represented a small portion of those watching this phenomena.

I awoke with perspiration dripping from my face. Groggily resigning the dream to that of a useless nightmare I drifted back into a deep sleep only to be awakened by the Lord's voice defending the experience with a commanding, "This dream was of God."

During the second week of August of 1977, Jerry's parents unexpectedly asked if the girls would visit them a few days. Normally these things were pre-planned and usually the youngest girl had to be coaxed into leaving. This time they were ecstatic.

"Okay, Lord, what is it? What's up with Elvis?" I questioned, while recalling the people's inability to hear me call to them during the dream I'd received only a few nights earlier. His answer was no answer.

Through all of the obvious warnings of the past few weeks I asked Denise to begin praying with me more heavily for Elvis. "On August sixteenth Elvis *has* to be surrounded by intense prayer. I feel this strongly. It has to be. I don't know why, yet. The Lord has put that date in my mind for the past several days. That's near the anniversary of his mother's death, maybe that's it. I don't know. But there definitely has to be intense constant prayer surrounding him on that day. I can't emphasize it enough," I grappled to explain.

On Sunday, August fourteenth, our Sunday school teacher requested prayer for Elvis.

119

Another lady told me about a Bible in which Elvis' mother had supposedly written "God Save Elvis" only days prior to her death.

Pastor Hardcastle made a timely remark as he reflected, "I find when Satan has fought me the hardest is when God is getting ready to give me the greatest victory of my lifetime."

Rationally I knew that, but I hadn't been very rational during the past few days. Because victory seemed to be escaping my grip, and instead I'd become increasingly worried about the future.

To add to my apprehension, the Lord retraced everything I'd done concerning Elvis and then one thing at a time, with a commanding tone, He told me that He was responsible for it all. I hadn't done one thing to cause me to be ashamed or proud.

On the afternoon of August fifteenth, Jerry and I drove by Baptist Memorial Hospital in Kansas City.

Glancing toward the emergency room entrance and feeling a strange shudder, I nervously remarked, "Wonder if Elvis is in there? Maybe we should go wait on him. He ought to be here before the next twenty-four hours pass by anyway."

Trying to lift the feeling of impending disaster, I laughed self-consciously and added, "But that'd be in Memphis, wouldn't it?"

Darkness seemed to be closing in, even though it was clothed with God's guidance. The nagging feeling of knowing another message was being transmitted through an interruption of my physical reaction played on my mind. For several days, severe heart palpitations had affected me until my entire body involuntarily weaved back and forth. My only response was a continuing stream of prayer.

Finally Jerry inquired about my increased floor walking and frequent times of withdrawal into prayer accompanied by my own physical appearance.

I tensely explained, "I can't pinpoint it, but it looks as far as Elvis and I are concerned, it's 'till death do us part'."

The night of August fifteenth I gripped my pillow to shed an ocean of tears as I searched desperately for something unfulfilled to claim. Something to grasp and be able to bring my insecurity to an end.

But there were no visions left unfulfilled, no promises that God had made about Elvis that He hadn't granted. Absolutely nothing was left to claim, except God's help in time of trouble and His standing promise to get Elvis safely to Heaven, coupled with the facts I now had after four years of labor.

I couldn't even remind the Lord that Elvis had a call to fulfill, because He'd never told me that Elvis would preach. He'd only told me that Elvis had been called.

16

THY WILL BE DONE

Dawn arrived with Elvis' name pulsating through my mind, along with a dream I'd had during the night. This feeling of extreme urgency caused me to forget that this was August sixteenth. The day I'd told Denise that Elvis would need more prayer than ever before.

As I became more aware of God's presence, the occurrences of the dream moved through my mind.

Elvis and another girl had been in a room. Entering a side door, and as always, not wanting to intrude, I turned to walk down a stairway nearby. Stopping momentarily, I leaned against the railing long enough to ask God for help. As usual, with the slightest prayer, Elvis turned toward me and began crying. Walking over to me he knelt on the second step.

This time I prayed desperately for the Lord to intervene by opening Elvis' spiritual eyes to see the danger he was facing. I awoke as it ended.

Before I'd gotten up the Lord had told me to begin "pleading the blood of Jesus," over Elvis. (Referring to the complete victory won on Calvary when Satan's final defeat came as the blood of Christ was spilled in this supreme act of sacrifice. Christians plead the blood of Jesus in times of uncertainty, knowing that this is the one weapon Satan can't penetrate.)

I made my way into the living room breathing out short, desperate pleas for Divine intervention.

In a dazed state, I walked toward the stereo to play Elvis' new album, hoping that it might in some way ease my pain and awaken me from this living nightmare.

But, instead, I became increasingly restless as the first strains of "Unchained Melody" filled the room. The sound was flat . . . no tonal quality . . . no three-dimensional effect . . . nothing. Yet, I'd played it before and it was fine.

Sensing that it had something to do with the way I'd felt during the past few days, I jerked the record off the turn table. Turning toward Heaven I voiced my worst fears, "It's dead, Lord! It's dead. It's just dead and gone . . . and there's no life left in it anymore."

Turning to run from the nagging reality of what I'd heard myself say, I ran outside slamming the door behind me. Leaning against the rail, I watched the rain slowly falling from gray, drab storm clouds. How appropriate.

Yielding to the urgency of the moment, I began petitioning God while the rain shed tears for me, "Move Elvis. Move him like You've never moved him, Lord. Now before it's too late! Reveal Yourself to him in power! This is it, Lord. Today. Right now. This is it," I implored. "I know distance is nothing with You. You've reached him regardless of where he's been. Talk to him, Lord."

While I prayed, Jerry came home unexpectedly. Slowly approaching me, he asked, "What's wrong with you? You're white as a sheet."

Dazed, I looked up and stumbling for an appropriate answer said, "It's you. I need to be alone today. I've just got to be alone and pray. I've just got to pray . . . all day. I don't know what's wrong, but I know it's Elvis. And I know this is it . . . today."

He disappeared into the house to let me alone with my thoughts.

Mid-afternoon as the phone rang, I recognized the same lifeless quality that I'd heard from the record that morning.

By now, I wasn't sure if I was going insane or something was drastically wrong. As I started toward the phone, I hesitated and turned to Jerry saying, "Just be sure and catch me before I hit the floor!"

His expression proved he didn't understand my hasty request.

With an inner dread, I picked up the receiver. Jan's emotionally-strained voice met me with an anxious, "Mary Ann? This is Jan . . . in Cincinnati. Have you heard?"

My mind raced in ten directions at once. It's Elvis, I thought. He's hurt. That stupid airplane he's always been afraid of has crashed. Maybe he's had a heart attack. Maybe that was the warning. Gathering my courage, I asked, "Heard what, Jan? What's wrong? What is it?"

"It's Elvis, Mary Ann. He's dead . . . he's gone. Mary Ann, he's gone," she repeated as her voice trailed off.

"Oh, God, no! Jan, it can't be," I argued, realizing I was challenging reality.

"It is, Mary Ann," she replied in a stern tone that only echoed her sincerity. "It's true. He's gone now."

"Okay," I strained to ask, knowing I'd have to hear the facts. "When did it happen?"

"Not long ago. They just found him a little while ago. I just heard and I had to call you," she said.

Jerry heard my questioning and asked what was wrong. I managed to utter the only two words that mattered, "Elvis died."

As I collapsed into a crumpled heap, he unbelievingly replied with a weak, "What did you say?"

In the midst of all my wanting to withdraw from humanity I knew two things. One, Elvis knew everything now. The things I never shared with him, death had brought a perfect knowledge of that and everything else the last four years had meant. And two, I had to go to Memphis. Ever since April 21, 1976, I'd told Jerry when Elvis died I'd have to go to Memphis and see for myself, or I'd never be able to accept it.

I phoned Denise to ask if she could go with me. Her first reaction was shock, although she knew I'd never believe something like that unless it was true. Then she began quoting Scriptures and telling me how the Lord had had her praying all day. Her words were comforting, but I wasn't hearing a single one.

My mother phoned as soon as she heard. "I suppose you're going to Memphis now," she said, "I heard about Elvis immediately after I turned the radio on. It surprised me, but it didn't surprise me. All night last night I was kept awake watching a lady dressed in mourning clothes with a black veil over her face. Throughout the night she stood looking south and wringing her hands cautioning, 'A beloved one will be gone'."

Although there weren't any rooms available in Memphis because of conventions and Elvis' funeral, the Lord miraculously provided a place to stay with Christians.

As we drove past Graceland, I saw, for the first time in all our trips to Memphis, the field north of his home that had been "flaming but not consumed" in the vision I'd had two years earlier.

Every tree was the same, the crowd and the news media

was there, Denise and I were there, and something had definitely happened to Elvis.

That first night we were in Memphis the Lord intruded into my unhappiness long enough to show me a vision of a beautiful American eagle.

His black and white plummage seemed to glisten in a radiant light. The vision of the molting brown eagle I'd seen in Las Vegas immediately came to mind. Now I knew that the entire change had occurred.

Incidentally, it takes an eagle approximately four years to obtain its mature plummage. Exactly the length of time I'd prayed for Elvis.

Never had I seen such an overall feeling of grief as was evident in Memphis. The entire city seemed draped in a cloak of mourning, somehow strangely resembling a preview of Judgment Day.

On August seventeenth, the public was allowed to view Elvis' body. As the gates swung shut at the end of that allotted time, one woman dramatically added, "I sure hope the Pearly Gates don't swing shut like those just did!"

The following day was the funeral. It was really a "happening." The people, the media, the helicopters and police all seemed to make a person realize that this wasn't simply a funeral, it was history.

The almost 100,000 people there were emotionally shattered for the most part.

I cried too, for God and Elvis, and myself as well, I suppose. And for all those things that might never be . . . not now.

Denise and I prayed with many people who were worse off than we were. I saw several friends and acquaintances, regardless of their names and prominence, their expressions all registered the same look of shocking reality.

Ed Parker, another of Elvis' friends, and I contacted each other where we could finally talk. But the words we grasped for were incapable of relating our feelings.

"He didn't have to go, Ed," I quietly reflected, "He didn't have to go."

"I know," he replied, embracing me as one would a fellow sympathizer. "No one wanted it this way."

Four days later, Denise and I returned home, tired, spiritually exhausted, and aware of a new realm of God's power.

When I reached home I phoned Jerry's sister, Sandy, and asked her to recall the dream she had received four years before of a building with white columns and double doors that she had thought was Graceland.

"Yes, I remember it," she replied. "The one where the Lord told me Elvis would be saved."

"That's the one. I've an idea, but I need the description first," I hurriedly related.

As I listened she meticulously described the mausoleum at Forrest Hills where Elvis had been entombed.

The next weekend Jerry and I made a visit to Memphis so he could see Elvis' grave.

The morning we were to leave, I was awakened from a deep sleep to see an open vision of a black-haired man dressed in pure white raiment silhouetted in an emerald green field, gazing over a cliff toward me. In the background loomed white architecture that appeared to have been carved from pure ivory. Instantly knowing it was Heaven, I began straining for a better look at the man.

Startled by the fact that I recognized him I quickly quizzed, "Lord, is that Elvis? Can that be him? Oh, Lord, You wouldn't let me see him now," I said, doubting what my own eyes were seeing. "But . . . he looks different than he did here! He looks peaceful and content. His face has the same look of those angels You've let me see. Oh, Lord, is that Elvis?"

In a calm, reassuring tone, the Lord patiently replied, "Yes, Mary Ann, that's Elvis. And, of course, he looks different. That's Heaven."

After Jerry and I arrived in Memphis the next day, we walked to the mausoleum, took pictures and reflected on the past.

On the way out of Forrest Hills, a young man from Youth for Christ was diligently passing out Gospel message pins. We talked to him and I mentioned that I'd known Elvis and he'd been called to be an evangelist although it'd never been done.

Slowly turning his eyes heavenward, then to the people streaming in and out of the cemetery to visit Elvis' grave and finally back to me reflecting, "You know something! You can't ever tell what he might be doing right now. Him and Jesus."

I stood in awe, realizing that he was awakening me to a fact I'd failed to consider until now.

Sadly, it was a long way from where Elvis stood to stepping behind a pulpit, and he viewed that distance with more severity than any one of us could. He alone knew his own limitations as well as his binding restrictions.

The transition wouldn't have been difficult for God. But it might have proven too much for Elvis. And God promises He won't put on any of us anymore than we can bear or our faith can accept.

Elvis knew what he should do and what was needed. Yet he feared rejection by the very people who cared the most . . . his fans.

He knew that the end of the age is near, although he stated in his own words that he was, "incapable of telling it."

If he had a chance to start over I know what he'd do and say because he knows people would listen and maybe now we realize that we would have listened as well.

For you see, Elvis' massive insecurity about being accepted at something besides a rock and roll singer has been shattered by only a glance into Jesus' tender all-knowing eyes.

And although he lost in one way, he won in others . . . because God won. Because now Elvis has something he searched for and longed to have . . . freedom.

If Elvis could return to make one final statement I'm sure he'd be first in line to point each of us firmly to the Promised Land that he has found after an exhausting search. I'm not condemning him because he searched. I'm praising God because He found Elvis and because Elvis listened when He did.

The Lord repeatedly tells us in His Word that He won't leave us comfortless no matter what happens. I believe that's one purpose of the release of this story. The countless number of Christians and fans that prayed for Elvis through the years deserve to receive that consolation. So accept this as words of assurance that God had everything under control.

One of the last things Elvis indicated to me before he died was how desperately he wanted to tell people that the Lord is our only answer. In his absence, allow me to convey that brief request on to you.

Walking through the mountains that I was shown at the beginning of this journey, I've found that storms prevail on the slopes. This has proven true in the physical as well as the spiritual. Storms have entered into this story through warnings and various other occurrences. Even Elvis seemed to mention them repeatedly. But in the midst of each tempest, I've heard God's commanding voice speak, "Peace, be still."

For, you see, faith to continue, regardless of how black the night, is necessary. Because eventually dawn will break forth and with it, joy in the morning, when all things are perfected in Christ.

In actuality, our brief sojourn on earth is only a metamorphic stage on the way to everlasting life. And our ability to understand the victory that death brings to us is limited on this side of Heaven where the child of God stands yearning for eternity to begin.

This temporal earthly kingdom we use as our launching pad into a thousand forevers will fade away like a daydream as we share the stories of how we escaped from this life into the true life where Jesus is the Light.

As we observe God's prophetic time clock we can see that it won't be long before we're there. His Word tells us that when we observe certain signs coming to pass upon the earth, to look up because our redemption draweth nigh (Luke 21:28).

My constant prayer and most sincere desire is that every person who has watched this journey unfold, as each stage was turned, will be present on that Resurrection Morning.